The
Strange
Case
of
Ambrose
Small

Fred McClement

The Strange Case of Ambrose Small

Illustrated with photographs

McClelland and Stewart Limited

0-7710-5498-X

The Canadian Publishers
McClelland and Stewart Limited
25 Hollinger Road, Toronto

Printed and bound in Canada

All photos in this book are reproduced
through the courtesy of *The Toronto Star*.

Chapter One

The old grandfather clock in the study chimed the hour of nine. The Honourable W.J. Shaughnessy slipped into his Melton overcoat and prepared to brave the winter winds between the side door of his palatial residence and his waiting limousine.

Ordinarily, the eminent financier would not have departed from his home at 659 Mountain Street until some forty-five minutes later to catch the Montreal-to-Toronto night train, which left at ten. But that night of Monday, December 1, 1919, was no ordinary night in Montreal. The city was in the icy grip of a wild winter storm, which was described by the newspapers as one of the worst in local meteorological history.

From four that afternoon, Montreal had been battered by the tail-end of a hurricane which on the previous day had ravaged Upper New York State and the Province of Ontario and was now churning up trouble northeastward along the broad valley of the St. Lawrence River. This untamed disturbance, which had started a week earlier in the tropics, collided with a bitter Arctic cold front over the confluence of the Ottawa and St. Lawrence rivers, and Montreal was reeling under swirling snow and tree-toppling winds.

The financier had no intention of missing that overnight train to Toronto. He had important business to transact the next morning as the representative of a large group of Montreal investors. Because he was a director of the Canadian Pacific Railway and Steamship Lines and his father, Baron Shaughnessy, was Chairman of the Board, a private railway car would be attached to the rear end of the train for his pleasure. He knew that authorities at the terminal would hold the entire train for him, for as long as fifteen minutes, if necessary. But W.J., as he was known throughout the coast-to-coast system, had a reputation for punctuality and no winter storm regardless of its fury would dare delay his date with destiny.

While his wife Marion was chattering over a number of forthcoming social engagements, which would begin the next night in Montreal, he kissed his three young daughters and an infant son farewell, pecked at his wife's cheek, and was immediately on his way down the twisting streets of the mountain toward the diffused glow of the downtown lights barely visible in the swirling mass. He arrived at the railway terminal ten minutes before the hour of departure and was accompanied to his coach by his chauffeur and a beaming stationmaster. It was just as well, as W.J. might have been embarrassed if a redcap had picked up his suitcase. He rarely carried money on his person and was known to have a passion against tipping, despite the fact that he was a member of one of the richest families in Canada and a senior partner in Montreal's largest legal firm dealing with international banking.

On this particular night, however, Shaughnessy was carrying one million dollars in his jacket pocket. It would be in his possession for twelve hours. Within twenty-four hours events of which he could have had no premonition would occur, with consequences that would involve churches, courts, police, governments, and the lives of scores of individuals over the next forty years.

Before retiring, he accepted a glass of Bristol Cream from

his porter and during this interlude he withdrew from his pocket a cashier's cheque: *Pay to the order of Ambrose J. Small the sum of one million dollars and no cents.*

He studied it, and returned the cheque to his pocket. He then retired, awoke at seven for breakfast, and was irritated by a message from the conductor that his train would not arrive at the Toronto Union Station until 9:15, more than an hour and a half behind schedule. The explanation for the delay was said to be the depth of snow along the mainline right-of-way.

In Toronto he was met by a C.P.R. official, but Shaughnessy desired to be alone. He turned to the right outside the terminal and walked briskly eastward along Front Street. His quick well-timed military step was the result of years of service in the Canadian Army; he had served as wartime aide to the Chief of Staff and was commanding officer of the Irish Rangers.

He crossed Bay Street, the main financial thoroughfare of Toronto, and continued on to Yonge Street. There he turned north on the east side, proceeded to Traders' Bank Building at 65 Yonge, and took the elevator to the Tenth Floor. Gold lettering on a bronze plate revealed the company: Aylesworth, Wright, Moss and Thompson, Attorneys at Law.

He was met by Sir Allen Aylesworth, K.C., the senior partner of the firm, who immediately led him to the board room where he was introduced to a man and a woman, both of them strangers to him. He bowed to a smiling Theresa Small and shook hands with her attorney, E. W. M. Flock. The latter conducted a law business on Market Lane in London, Ontario.

The principal person was missing. Ambrose Small never arrived anywhere on time. It was part of his peppery character to keep people waiting, and Shaughnessy showed his irritation by constantly referring to his Waltham pocket watch. It was ten after ten and Small was ten minutes late already.

At 10:45, Ambrose Small was ushered into the ornate panelled room behind a cloud of thick Havana smoke. After a cool introduction to Shaughnessy, Sir Allen called the meeting to order and proffered a lengthy legal document to Ambrose and Theresa with Flock looking over their shoulders. Theresa gave the papers only a slight glance and chatted and laughed with Shaughnessy. He thought she would have made an intelligent addition to the stuffy English society of Montreal. He knew she was a leader of Toronto's select social order and he could not help but admire her. He noted that she was quick to respond with a smile. Her eyes were gay and bright, her clothes the latest in winter fashion.

Beyond the social status, he knew little of Theresa or her husband, other than that they owned a chain of theatres across the country and that Trans-Canada Theatres Limited, whom he represented, were at this moment presenting an offer to purchase the Small holdings for $1,700,000 with a down payment of one million and the balance to be paid in annual instalments without interest over the next five years.

While Flock and Ambrose Small were reading this offer, an interlude of tea-drinking gave Shaughnessy the opportunity to observe the man to whom he would shortly proffer the cashier's cheque. Ambrose Small did not have the appearance of a wealthy businessman. He could never have fitted the description of an impressive executive. Small was five feet six, weighing not more than 140 pounds. His eyes were bright blue and he had a reddish complexion with numerous broken veins on the cheeks, which Shaughnessy attributed to alcohol. His brown hair was greying at the temples and was combed neatly rearward and parted on the left side. His most dominant feature was a large walrus mustache that arched across his upper lip. The mustache was unwaxed at the ends and therefore most un-British, and Shaughnessy, a graduate of Trinity College,

Cambridge, and of McGill, knew that Small was nothing more than an upstart. He must have wondered how Theresa and Ambrose had ever come together but he had little time to ponder.

"Agreed," said Small. He affixed his name to the contract and Theresa did likewise. The signatures were witnessed by Flock, Aylesworth and Shaughnessy, and the latter handed Small the cheque for the million-dollar down payment.

Small looked at it, endorsed it, and blew a swirling cloud of smoke toward the ceiling. Everyone was beaming.

"Here, take it and put it in the bank . . . and don't spend it on the way over. That's a million in cash," he said to Theresa.

Her face wreathed in a smile, Theresa quickly left the board room and headed for the Dominion Bank. En route, she waved to her old friend, Frank Regan, a well-known Toronto criminal lawyer and a noted and well-respected Catholic layman in Protestant Toronto. Theresa showed him the cheque, his eyes popped open and a smile enveloped his jowled face. Theresa was the city's chief benefactress of the Diocese.

"Your husband must think an awful lot of you, Theresa!" Regan commented. "That's a million-dollar bill."

She invited the lawyer to luncheon but he declined; he had an appearance shortly at the City Hall Court and he took a "rain check" on the invitation.

Theresa then proceeded to the Dominion Bank where she startled the staff with the fantastic amount of the cheque. A million dollars in 1919 was a veritable fortune. It was also tax-free. The official record of the deposit was noted in the bank deposits of December 2. It was precisely 11:45 a.m.

Theresa left the bank and walked eastward along King Street to the King Edward Hotel, a matter of two blocks. In the lavish Victoria dining room she was served tea while she "patiently" waited for Flock and her tardy husband. The two men finally arrived at 12:30, and in a convivial mood. But Theresa was rarely angered and the euphoria of increasing her millions only added to her sparkling manner.

The luncheon completed, Theresa reminded Ambrose that he had promised to accompany her to the St. Vincent de Paul Children's Orphanage on Shuter Street, four blocks north of the King Edward. She was that day presenting a Christmas donation of several thousand dollars and she wanted Ambrose to share the occasion. It was a duty that Small hated. He had little use for the Catholic Church and he grumbled all the way north to the institution. But he had solemnly promised weeks earlier that if he sold the theatres he would assist his wife in the financial presentation, and he kept the promise but only because Theresa reminded him of his vow all the way over the snowy streets.

Small did not enjoy the company of children. It may have been because he was biologically incapable of fatherhood despite the fact that he had an international reputation for sexual prowess, about which Theresa had been hearing more and more in the past few months. She had actually discussed the gossip of extramarital sex with members of her family but if any decision had been reached on the delicate matter, there is no evidence that family action was contemplated.

When the duties at the orphanage were completed, Ambrose promised to be home at the couple's mansion on Glen Road, in the snobby Rosedale district of Toronto, "around six." The supper was to be a celebration of the theatre-chain sale. Theresa was driven home by the family chauffeur and Ambrose walked one block west to Yonge Street and then south toward his office in the Grand Opera House on Adelaide Street, a connecting street between Yonge and Bay in the very centre of the inner city. He was to meet Flock again at four o'clock to discuss the disposition of the theatre, now that the sale had been completed and he was no longer in command.

As usual, Small was late and Flock fretted, as he had to catch the six o'clock Canadian National Maple Leaf for London because of a bar association meeting that night. From the Grand Opera House to the Union Station was a distance of slightly more than three city blocks and Flock had calculated that it would take him at least fifteen minutes to make the run, taking into consideration the snow and the icy condition of the streets. It was faster to walk rapidly to the station than to depend on a horse-drawn street car at that time of year.

While Flock paced back and forth in the foyer, W.J. Shaughnessy was seated in his private railway car watching the activity of the Toronto yards as his Montreal-bound train cleared the terminal. A few miles to the north, Theresa Small was chauffeured from her home to join her sister Josephine in a shopping expedition. She mentioned that Ambrose would never have to work again and the two of them could spend their remaining years in travelling around the world.

It was now 4:20 p.m.

Back at the Opera House, Flock knew that Small had arrived by the pungent smell of cigar smoke being wafted by the draft of the street door opening. Small was in a bright mood, a sharp contrast to his usual grumpy, teeth-grinding manner.

It brightened Flock's own mood but he reminded Ambrose that he could not miss the London train and Small laughed the matter away, saying that the final details to be worked out would take less than an hour.

Why had Small been late? None of his friends and associates had ever heard him give an explanation. But on this afternoon of December 2, he broke with tradition, such was the effect of the sale on his emotions. Small told Flock that on his walk from the Orphanage to the Grand, he stopped at two places. At Toronto Cadillac he ordered a limousine for Theresa worth nine thousand dollars. Two blocks farther south, he ordered a huge pearl and diamond necklace from Kent's jewellery store.

He said the necklace cost "in the neighbourhood of ten thousand dollars."

"Why not," beamed his attorney.

"Why not," Small agreed.

The two now bent over Small's desk to work out the employment problems that had evolved from the sale of theatres in Toronto, Montreal, London, Windsor, Vancouver and other Canadian cities. Small agreed without reluctance to pay one week's salary to each employee with a promise that he would try to find them new positions, either with Trans-Canada or elsewhere. He blandly assigned this task to Flock, who winced at the thought. One person would be retained in the change-over: John Doughty, Small's secretary, would be absorbed by the new company and Small would tell him about it that very afternoon.

Doughty had been a faithful secretary and booking manager for Small for some fifteen years, almost from the day Ambrose bought the Grand Opera House after the turn of the century. Despite reports that Small often treated his employees, including Doughty, with contempt and low wages, the contract with Trans-Canada clearly contained a proviso that Doughty would continue in his position as a secretary and booking agent but with two changes: his salary would be increased, and his new office would be in Montreal.

Flock jumped. It was almost 5:30 p.m. The actual discussions with Small had taken slightly more than an hour. Small walked with Flock to the glass doorway at the entrance of the foyer. Still exuberant over becoming a multi-millionaire that day, he slapped the lawyer on the back and offered him a cigar, which Flock refused, as he did not smoke. They parted in good spirits.

Flock turned, as soon as he reached the sidewalk. He could see Small in the doorway and he waved farewell.

Then, through the whipping snow, he sprinted to the Union Station.

Chapter Two

Street lights glowed in the snowy darkness beyond the shadowy stone and brick of 51 Glen Road. In the music room which overlooked the tree-lined street and the wide family driveway, Theresa Small waited for her husband's arrival in his own limousine. The Westminster chimes in the rotunda of the mansion announced the time. It was 6:30 p.m.

Supper was planned for seven o'clock, and Catherine Dunn, the cook, was in the kitchen at the rear of the house preparing a special menu for the occasion. In the dining room a large bouquet of flowers, newly arrived from the florist's, graced the centre of a large ornate table cloaked in white and set with sterling silver. Clusters of candles cast their flickering shapes on the sombre oak panels of the four walls and reflected their brightness from the French windows that overlooked the snow-covered precision of the back gardens.

But Theresa really knew better than to expect Ambrose at the promised time. At seven, she told the cook to hold back the main course as it was now evident the couple could not possibly begin the celebration supper until sometime after eight. Ambrose always liked a number of stiff drinks before his evening meal.

At 7:30, she heard a noise in the basement and she called down to Harry Hadrill, the furnaceman, to increase the heat from the boilers as the vast sixteen-room home required an over-abundance of heat through the system to maintain a livable climate during such cold weather. After talking to Hadrill, she returned to the music room. She dismissed the two maids for the night, and by eight o'clock she had told the cook that something must have happened to Ambrose to delay him on such an occasion. There must have been trouble at the theatre, where, at this moment, crowds would be gathering at the reservation and ticket windows for the exciting drama, *Revelations of a Wife*.

Ambrose, she knew, loved to pick daring and melodramatic slush for his theatres, and although she herself disliked such immoral interludes she fully realized that in the depressive atmosphere of post-war Toronto they were necessary to the continued success of the legitimate theatres. Although devoted to the Catholic's strict code of morality, Theresa never permitted her religious feelings to interfere with box-office receipts or with the selections of lurid and sexually-saucy melodramas that made the cash register ring.

Theresa, for reasons known only to herself, did not call the Grand Opera House until 10:30 that night, long after the cook had departed and the celebration supper had been packed away into the ice-box. The phone in the Grand office was answered by Percy Small, the stage manager, who had been given a position by a reluctant Ambrose and an insistent Theresa. Percy was the son of Theresa's sister, Josephine. Josephine was married to Ambrose's father, Daniel. This mix-up in family relationship was created when Ambrose married Theresa after his widowed father had married Josephine.

Had Percy seen Amby (as she called her husband)?

No, he had not.

Not at any time during the evening?

No.

Did he tell anyone he was going somewhere?

Percy said he would ask around, but until Theresa's phone

call, he said, he had been busy backstage, and not seeing Ambrose around was not unusual.

At eleven, Theresa phoned again and this time the receiver was picked up by James Cowan, the general manager. Asked if Amby was in the vicinity, Cowan replied that he had not seen him but that his crony Thomas Flynn was in the foyer and he would ask him to come to the phone. Flynn had not seen Amby either, and was irritated at the thought that Small had slipped away on a spree without telling him. In spite of that, he asked Theresa why she didn't leave Small alone and let him have a little fun.

Theresa hung up. She immediately went to her secluded shrine in the basement and prayed before the altar. Then she retired, according to the snooping maids who slept on the top floor. Flynn may have convinced her that Ambrose was "on the town" and if he had gone to his usual place he would be at Abe Orpen's gambling casino, located on the banks of the Humber River just outside the jurisdiction of the Toronto police.

Flynn was angered and he saw Percy Small locking the office for the night.

"Where the hell is Small?" demanded Flynn.

"How do I know?" retorted Percy in his best sarcastic manner; he had little use for Flynn, or for any man who spent his life gambling. Flynn was Commissioner of the Ontario Racing Commission and it was no secret that Small had made hundreds of thousands of dollars at the races from tips supplied to him by Flynn.

"Where's Doughty, goddammit!"

"He should be on his way to Montreal right now . . . and he won't be back."

"And why not?"

"Mr. Small sold his theatres today."

Flynn's jaw dropped. "Where could the little bastard be?"

he thought out loud. Percy turned his back and continued with his duties of closing the Grand for the night.

There was a private line to Orpen's which was used often to tip the gambling czar that a provincial police raid was imminent, and Flynn had the secret number. Orpen stated that Small had not shown up at the tables and he was a little surprised. He suggested that Flynn try one of Small's more intimate friends, but Flynn, annoyed at the slight of being passed by on the night of the celebration, had a drink next door and then went home. He could have called Clara Smith, a girl whom he had introduced to Small as an evening companion. But he didn't. He went straight home to the comfort of his easy chair and his liquor cabinet.

The next day, December 3, Flynn was at the Grand when Percy arrived to open it.

"Have you seen Ambrose?" queried Flynn.

"No, and neither has Theresa."

"Aren't you concerned?" snapped Flynn.

"Not at all, Mr. Small may be celebrating."

"Jesus Christ, without his friends?"

"I wouldn't know that. . . . I do not associate with Mr. Small's friends."

Flynn stormed from the Opera House only minutes before Theresa arrived. She talked briefly with Percy and then returned to Glen Road.

Flynn returned to the theatre on December 4th and bumped into James Cowan. He learned from Cowan that Ambrose had disappeared into thin air and Cowan expressed the opinion that his boss might have gone to Florida to follow the racing season.

"He wouldn't have done that without telling me," growled Flynn, who hung around the theatre all that day and returned briefly day after day until December 16 when he decided to rouse some official action in the case. He drove to Toronto police headquarters on Court Street and asked to speak to Chief Inspector George Guthrie. He told him he wanted to report a missing person and Guthrie, preoccupied with other duties, did not inquire the name of the missing person but turned Flynn over to Detective Austin Mitchell, who was reading the latest issue of the naughty *Police Gazette* when Flynn entered the cubbyhole.

"I want to report a missing person."

Mitchell yawned. This happened several times a day. He pulled a "Missing Persons Record" from his desk drawer and asked the name.

"Ambrose J. Small," said Flynn.

"You don't mean the millionaire?" Mitchell casually replied.

"Oh yes, I do!"

Mitchell lowered his feet to the floor and looked hard at Flynn. "How long has he been missing?"

"Since the second of December."

"Why hasn't his wife informed us, if this is a fact?"

"How should I know? . . . Go and find out, that's your job."

"What about his friends, his girl friends?"

"I am his best pal, and as far as I know and unless he's welching on me, he has only one gal friend and she's as worried as I am."

Mitchell looked at Flynn quizzically. "If it's the same Ambrose Small I'm thinking of, he's got a reputation around town."

"So what?" retorted Flynn. "He sure as hell is missing. His wife hasn't seen him, his father hasn't heard from him, none of his staff has seen him, and by Jesus, two weeks is a long time."

Mitchell told Flynn to cool down, that it was more than likely Small had taken off for the sunny south and was probably at one of the race tracks in Florida where he was a familiar figure. It was no secret to Flynn that Small kept tab on every race track in the United States, usually by following the weekly listings in the Sunday edition of the *New York Times*. While Mitchell promised to make contact with the Small family, Flynn, who knew every major bookie in the city, started making phone inquiries to learn if Small had placed any bets since December 2. He had not. In fact, Small's favourite bookie, Pete Frealey, said that Small had not placed any bets in the system since sometime in late November and he attributed this to Small's visit to Montreal.

Flynn knew that Ambrose had been in Montreal just prior to the sale of his theatres and his preoccupation with the negotiations might have kept him from his usual study of the thoroughbred races. Flynn returned to his residence on Farnham Avenue and started calling various clubs where Ambrose would appear from time to time for luncheons or business engagements. He called the National Club, the Ontario Jockey Club, the Canadian Club and others. No Ambrose Small. Flynn's anger at his pal was turning into fear. He knew that Small had enemies. Plenty of them. Every gambler had enemies and Small was a big gambler and would take a bet on almost anything as long as it was a challenge with favourable odds to win. He called Mitchell and was informed that the detective had left for the Small residence on Glen Road.

Mitchell had attempted to phone Theresa but was told by one of the maids that Theresa was not answering the phone to anyone. Theatre manager Cowan had tried to reach her for ten days and she had not answered him. However, when the maid was informed that Mitchell was a police officer, he was told to come to the house and Theresa would speak to him. He arrived at the mansion at approximately three o'clock.

It was Theresa herself who admitted the officer. One of the maids took his heavy winter coat and his grey fur hat, as he was not in uniform. Theresa invited him to afternoon tea, and

Mitchell broached the subject of Ambrose's absence from the Toronto scene.

"His friends are worried," Mitchell informed her.

Then Theresa confided to Mitchell that her husband had been "running around" with chorus girls who were members of the stage presentation at the Opera House and she had the name of at least one woman with whom Ambrose had been dallying. "My husband is in the hands of a designing woman," she told Mitchell. "If this should reach the newspapers, the scandal would destroy me."

Theresa was crying. Mitchell nodded his head; he understood the situation. Theresa was an officer in the Imperial Order Daughters of the Empire, the most influential social force in Toronto. She was also an active member of the Toronto Ladies' Club, the Women's Art Association of Toronto, the Women's Canadian Club, the Women's Canadian Historical Society and the Musical Club of Toronto. A scandal could certainly create problems for a woman as prominent as Theresa in the social life of the city.

It was already dark when Mitchell took his leave, and he went straight home. When he came to his office the next morning, he did not make a report of his visit to Theresa. He later defended this omission to Guthrie by saying that he had feared some snoopy newspaper reporter would see the report and create a lurid story from it. However, when Flynn telephoned the next day, Mitchell said that he had information that Ambrose was on an out-of-town spree and would probably show up at Christmas.

"It won't be Christmas that would make him come back," commented Flynn. "Ambrose never gave anything to anyone in his life, except to Theresa and his bloody barber."

Mitchell just laughed. "Wait and see," he said, and hung up.

But Small did not come back to town on Christmas, nor was he seen over the New Year's holiday. Flynn thought he knew Ambrose better than any person alive, knew his habits, his escapades with women, his haunts, his cronies, yet all his checks had failed to find even the faintest trace of his friend. What bothered him most was the attitude of Theresa and Percy Small, their lack of alarm and the fact that social standing seemed more important to them than personal concern. Small's girl, Clara Smith, hadn't seen him for over a month. Nor had she heard from him.

Flynn called the City Desk at the *Toronto Daily Star* on the afternoon of January 2, 1920, one month from the day that Small disappeared. He did not bother to call the *Evening Telegram*, nor the *Globe*, nor the *Mail and Empire*. A staunch Roman Catholic, he despised all Toronto newspapers except the *Star*, as it was the only daily that gave the minorities in the city any kind of a fair break.

Harry Hindmarsh was assistant managing editor. He knew a good story when he saw one and immediately assigned three reporters to follow up the tip. He sent one reporter to police headquarters to talk to Chief Inspector George Guthrie. Guthrie didn't know anything about it. Hindmarsh assigned another reporter to track down Small's associates, and another he sent to Small's residence. Then he spent a sleepless night, concerned that one of the morning papers might scoop a great story. It was always hot news when a millionaire vanished.

On the morning of January 3, Hindmarsh was at his desk in the *Star*'s editorial offices when the *Globe* and the *Mail and Empire* were brought to him. There was no mention of the Small disappearance. Meanwhile his reporters had ferreted enough information to make an international story. For the *Star* he ordered an eight-column streamer across the top of the front page:

WELL-KNOWN THEATRICAL MAGNATE
HAS NOT BEEN SEEN FOR FIVE WEEKS
WHEN LAST SEEN—IN BEST OF HEALTH

The whereabouts of Mr. Ambrose J. Small, one of Canada's most prominent theatrical men, is causing gravest concern to his relatives and business associates. Mr. Small was last seen in Toronto on December 2, 1919 after he had closed the sale of his vast theatrical holdings to the Trans-Canada Theatres Limited, and had received a very large cheque as initial payment.

The Star interviewed Mr. E.W.M. Flock, of London, Ontario, Mr. Small's attorney by long distance telephone this morning who said: "I left Mr. Small in his office about 5:30 p.m. on Tuesday, December 2nd. and further than that I know nothing about him. He had closed up the sale of his Grand Opera circuit, six houses in all, to the Trans-Canada Theatres Ltd. He closed with me, as his solicitor, later that day. He received the initial payment, which was a large sum of money and it was immediately deposited.

"I was with Mr. Small about an hour at his office and he was never more pleasant or genial and was full of pep and vim. I told him I might be down to see him the following week. I have been to Toronto two or three times since then, but have been told that he was not at the office. As in cases of this kind newspapers are invaluable in locating a man, I see no reason why I should not tell you what I have."

Police Making Inquiries.

Inspector Guthrie of the Toronto Detective Department, when interviewed by the Star said: "We are making inquiries all around, but have found nothing yet."

Completed Big Deal.

On Saturday, November 29, Mr. Small got back to Toronto from Montreal, where he had agreed to the sale of all his theatrical interests, including the above-mentioned to a syndicate incorporated as the Trans-Canada Theatres Ltd. Tuesday he received a marked cheque for a million dollars on account of the transaction.

He met Mrs. Small downtown and after lunch went for a short distance with her and returned to his office in the Grand Opera House, where he met Mr. E.W.M. Flock, barrister, of London, who had been his legal adviser in the transaction closed the previous week in Montreal. Mr. Flock went out on the street about half-past five. That is the last known so far of Mr. Small in Toronto. No trace of him of any kind since that date, four weeks ago, can be found.

For a few days Mrs. Small and his assistants at the Grand Opera House imagined that he had been called suddenly to one of the out-of-town theatres or to Montreal, and some days later on when no word had come from him that perhaps he had gone to New York on pressing business. This suspense continued for two weeks then a third and for a fourth week.

Search Was Made.

A quiet but diligent search of the city, including hospitals and hotels, stations, and the like was made by the police, fearing that he might be ill.

It is remarkable that as far as is known Mr. Small had with him at the time of his disappearance no luggage or clothes other than those he wore and it is not believed that he had much money upon his person.

Mr. Small is a very wealthy man and is believed to have

bank accounts with large balances. But an examination of these showed no withdrawals made or attempted by anyone.

Mr. Small was naturally of a nervous temperament and for several months he had been working long hours at the task of arranging the details of many and varied phases of his business that had to be settled in order to bring about the theatrical amalgamation which he desired to effect. He was an exceedingly keen businessman, and knew personally every detail of his affairs. Towards the end of the negotiations he worked far into the night and had latterly complained of nervous exhaustion and loss of appetite.

The hope is, however, that the publicity started by this announcement will result in the discovery of Mr. Small's whereabouts. The photograph reproduced herewith is an old one. It is an excellent portrait of Mr. Small but since it was taken he has worn his mustache shortly clipped. With the exception of that change it should greatly help in his identification.

Said He Would Take Rest.

Montreal, Que. Jan. 3—George F. Driscoll, general manager of Trans-Canada Theatres Ltd. this morning said that he had seen or heard nothing of Mr. Small after cleaning up the theatrical deal. He stated, however, that in the course of the last conversation he had with him at the meeting when the deal was put through Mr. Small said that he would now go away for a rest. Mr. Driscoll said that Mr. Small never carried any money on him, drawing a cheque whenever he needed it.

Chief Inspector Guthrie was on the spot. There was no report of the Small disappearance in the Toronto Police Department's

Missing Persons' file, although Flynn had now told reporters that he announced the disappearance on December 16th. It was mandatory that all police officers record all telephone calls and personal visits to the police and all investigations, no matter how minor, and Guthrie could find no entry in the files that Flynn had called or that any check had been made into the disappearance.

When Mitchell returned to his desk on January 5, Guthrie was fuming.

"Where the hell is the Small report?" he demanded. "Every Goddamned newspaper in the country is asking about Ambrose Small . . . where is the report?"

"I did not make a report on his disappearance because it would have been embarrassing to Mrs. Small," Mitchell confessed. "Small has been celebrating the theatre sale and his family is convinced he'll be back in town soon. Why stir up a stink?"

"You're right," said Guthrie. "There's no reason to suspect foul play. The least we can do is to save his wife the embarrassment of his celebration."

"Small is celebrating, and why not," Guthrie told the newspapers, and immediately an air of frivolity enveloped the disappearance. A drunk falling on his face in the street would bring the jeer of a passer-by: "It must be Ambrose Small."

Telephone calls, postcards and letters descended on police headquarters from hundreds of quacks and queers, as well as from scores of serious-minded persons, announcing that Ambrose had been seen and identified in many places around the city. Calls also came from cities in the United States and even from as far away as Mexico. Sifting all this information became an impossible job, and Mitchell turned to local clairvoyants to help him solve his problems.

Mitchell was a man who believed in extra-sensory perception. It was almost a joke around headquarters that when Gypsies came to town, Mitchell was one of the first to seek crystal-ball advice. He believed in teacup reading, playing-card manipulations, star signs and mysticism. He told his associates that he had managed to solve crimes in the past by talking with mediums on the behaviour and attitudes of criminals. He believed that if a man was a gambler, he was automatically a crook and ne'er-do-well; it didn't matter that nothing was logged in the crime files. He therefore considered Small to be a man on the periphery of the law.

Mitchell's attitude at this time was still one of "He's a rich bum. Let's wait and see what happens." Apparently Guthrie agreed with Mitchell, since he kept him on the case, exclusively.

But the *Toronto Star* reporters added a second mystery to the first. By interrogation of people who knew Small, they discovered that his secretary John Doughty had also disappeared. He had shown up in Montreal about the 3rd of December by reporting for duty at Trans-Canada Theatres. Then, at Christmastime, he had been given a vacation to visit his family in Toronto with the understanding that he would report back for work in Montreal on December 29. He had not returned. A quick check with his sister Jeannie at her River Street address showed that Doughty had indeed been back in Toronto at Christmastime and had left again for Montreal. Now, Jeannie as well as Doughty's two young boys, whom Jeannie cared for, were worried.

The mystery deepened and Austin Mitchell was shocked because the disappearance of Small's ex-secretary had not been predicted by the clairvoyants.

In any event, Mitchell and Guthrie became convinced there was a relationship between Small's disappearance and Doughty's but this only heightened their belief that Small had "taken off" to celebrate his good fortune and had taken his long-time pal and secretary with him, to share the fun. This reasoning was supported by a press report over the international wire system of the Associated Press that Harry Blackstone, the famous magician, had recently seen Ambrose Small in a gambling casino in Juarez, Mexico.

Blackstone was located by Mitchell performing in a Chicago supper club, and a telegram asked him for further details of the incident. Blackstone, who was a familiar performer in Toronto, replied that he had known Small for many years and "recently in Juarez, I saw Amby playing at the tables and I called out his name and waved to him. . . . I shouted 'Hi Amby' but when I attempted to get over to him, Small ran out the door."

An all-points bulletin was circulated throughout the United States, as well as Canada, describing Small's characteristics in great detail, even to the fact that Small had hammertoes on both feet. This immediately led to derisive conjectures that he had been born with webbed feet and had swum away someplace. Small's hammertoes received great attention on the vaudeville stages of both countries and the disappearance became associated with fun and laughter instead of the seriousness it deserved.

Chapter Three

It was Thomas Flynn's relentless badgering of Guthrie, who in turn nagged Mitchell into broadening the investigation, that kept the case alive. Mitchell was expected to have reports on all friends and associates of the missing tycoon. Every place of business in downtown Toronto was to be personally checked by Mitchell to ascertain whether or not Small was known to have business with each firm, and, if so, when was the last time he had made purchases or had services. And Mitchell dutifully plodded from place to place like a bloodhound on the trail, interrogating the barber, checking the taverns and the bartenders, questioning the waiters where Small traditionally dined, the downtown garages where his limousine was often parked, florist shops in particular to learn if Small had ordered flowers for persons other than Theresa, jewellery stores to ascertain whether gifts had been purchased or were on order for women other than his wife.

It was a long gruelling search, from morning until night, seven days a week. Mitchell was a familiar figure, knocking on doors, stopping persons on the street and huddled over a garage mechanic's tables, with the white writing-pad snapped open at a new page for each new person interviewed. Mitchell learned that Small was well known by sight but other than that, a man of mystery who confided in no one and conversed rarely except with business and financial friends. His gambling cronies melted from sight any time that Mitchell appeared on the scene. It was a frustrating case at every turn.

Theresa Small provided Guthrie with a photograph of her husband taken a number of years before his disappearance. She remarked that he had gained a little weight and had trimmed the walrus mustache slightly. Otherwise, it was a good likeness. The photograph was distributed to all police departments in Canada and the United States, and to major cities around the world, together with a description and the offer of a reward:

> *I am authorized by Mrs. Ambrose J. Small and Capital Trust Corporation to offer a reward of $50,000 for information leading to the discovery of the present whereabouts of the above named man, if alive.*
>
> *Description: Age 53, 5ft. 6 or 7 ins; 135 to 140 pounds. Blue eyes, sallow complexion. Brown hair and moustache, streaked with grey. Hair receding at temples. Is very quick in his movements.*
>
> *Mr. Small, who is well known in theatrical circles in the United States and Canada, was owner of the Grand Opera House, Toronto, and was last seen in his office at this theatre on the afternoon of December 2nd, 1919.*
>
> *When last seen he was wearing a dark tweed suit and dark overcoat with velvet collar and a soft felt hat. The above photo, although taken some time ago, is a good likeness, except that for a considerable time previous to his disappearance he had been wearing his mustache clipped short.*
>
> *I am also authorized to offer in the alternative, a reward of $15,000 for information leading to the discovery of the present whereabouts of the body of the above named man, if dead.*
>
> *The information must be received before September 1st,*

1920, on which date the above offers of rewards will expire.
All previous offers of rewards are withdrawn.
Wire all information to the undersigned,

H. J. Grasett
Chief Constable

Police Headquarters,
TORONTO
June 1st, 1920

A reward of this magnitude attracted scores of detectives from both sides of the border to the Toronto scene. Together with newsmen, they turned up a number of important clues, one of which was the fact that John Doughty possessed the keys to Small's safety-deposit boxes at the Dominion Bank. When Mitchell tried to examine the records of the bank, the authorities refused all information and it took a court order to examine the records. It was learned that Doughty went to the vault, where the safety-deposit boxes were contained, on December 2nd and removed $100,000 in negotiable bonds from Small's box. He had signed his name to the removal before a bank witness, which was mandatory for any trusted person acting on behalf of a superior. Doughty had that authority.

Where were the bonds? Mitchell and Guthrie were puzzled. Was Doughty a thief? Or had he taken out the bonds for Ambrose, to finance his disappearance? Were the two men together? Because he wasn't sure, Guthrie issued a "Wanted" bulletin on Doughty and, with a photograph attached and the offer of a $15,000 reward, sent it to all police headquarters on both sides of the border.

One thing was bothering Guthrie but he did not discuss this with Mitchell because he noticed that his detective was more apt to protect Theresa against possible scandal than to regard her objectively as one of several persons involved in a mystifying situation. Guthrie was well aware of Theresa's charm and her powerful social position in the city and he could well understand that Mitchell, if drawn into her orbit, might overlook possible criminal evidence or, at least, some evidence that might help in finding the two men.

Guthrie's concern centred on the mystery of the missing bonds. Could Doughty have removed them without Theresa's knowledge? Within a day or so of Small's disappearance, wouldn't it have been logical for Theresa to check his safety-deposit boxes to see if the bonds or other valuables had been removed? Wouldn't this have provided some support to the theory that he had run away? As a partner in all his business affairs, wouldn't Theresa have been immediately concerned about $100,000 lying in a safety-deposit box?

Guthrie found himself linking Theresa to the missing bonds and to the disappearance of John Doughty. The more he thought about the link, the more he believed it to be possible. And if there was a Theresa-Doughty link, why not a connection between Theresa and the missing husband? Without telling Mitchell of his thoughts, Guthrie had a meeting with Ontario's Attorney General and assigned to the case was Inspector C. D. Hammond of the c.i.b. The c.i.b. was the crime investigation branch of the Ontario Provincial Police. Its inspectors were assigned to municipal cases only on the request of a high police authority.

When Hammond and Mitchell met for the first time, there was instant hostility between them. Hammond called mind-readers, clairvoyants and palmists a "bunch of nuts." Mitchell was, at the moment, preparing a national advertisement asking for the help of the occult scientific world. Astrologers and supernatural experts were also asked to join in the search for Small and Doughty.

Hammond linked the disappearances as a planned combination and suspected no foul play. Where Mitchell thought that Small and Doughty would soon be found with women in their arms, Hammond thought there was a possibility that both men had changed their physical appearance and might never be found. He also told Mitchell there might be other Small safety-deposit boxes elsewhere in the city. Had he checked? Mitchell had not.

"We must check banks and savings houses in every city where Small had theatres," Hammond said. Mitchell asked for more help and was provided with six detectives from headquarters to check Toronto banks. Hammond would use the province-wide facilities of the Ontario Provincial Police to conduct a check-out of banks in London, Windsor, Niagara Falls, Peterborough, Kingston and Hamilton.

Mitchell could see that Hammond might get all the glory if the case were solved. He therefore kept a daily liaison with the Toronto newspaper reporters, who were assigned on a 24-hour basis to the Small enigma. The city was swarming with private investigators from all over the United States, and Mitchell co-operated with this unrestrained mob by keeping them posted on the day-to-day developments of the case.

Hammond smoked a pipe which Mitchell detested and their conversations became less frequent. Mitchell remained close to Theresa, and Hammond secretly placed an officer on her movements. Within days, the officer found that Theresa never left the Glen Road house at this period. Talking with one of her maids, he learned that Theresa spent many hours standing behind the music-room curtains watching the train of reporters and investigators troop to the front door, to be turned away by the weary servants. Hammond's plainclothesman reported that Percy Small, her nephew, was a frequent visitor, as was her sister Josephine. Others coming to the house included a number of Catholic priests and scores of nuns from several convents and novitiates in the city. Not one of them was interrogated at any time. Mitchell ordered that Theresa Small be given absolute privacy and if there was to be any questioning or discussion with her, he would be the man.

Inspector Guthrie sent his detectives in a fanning movement into downtown Toronto to check all places of business in a three-block area around the Grand Opera House. Hammond thought this was a waste of manpower but Guthrie was insistent. He believed that someone, other than the lawyer Flock, must have seen Small the afternoon of December 2. Small had bought a Cadillac and a necklace for Theresa. What else had he bought? Who else had Ambrose seen or talked with on his rare spending spree?

Guthrie had no use for Hammond's intelligence and was, on occasion, openly insulting to the Provincial officer. Guthrie knew that on Hammond's most recent investigation, the Inspector not only found no evidence of stock fraud against a prominent Toronto broker, who was suspected of bilking millions from unsuspecting American investors, but actually bought five thousand shares of the disputed stock himself, only to find later that the stock was worthless. The broker had fled to South America by the time Hammond discovered the fraud.

Guthrie expected little help from Hammond. He would give Mitchell broader powers and ask for increased funds for his 1920 budget. Reports were coming into Toronto headquarters from every major city in the States and some of them were important enough to track down by telephone. Such continuing reports of missing persons being found, dead and alive, would soon swell to a gigantic wave, and yet they could not be ignored.

Mouldy bodies were being dug up and hauled to police stations across both countries. Every time a drowning victim washed to shore, the body, often decomposed, would be dragged to the closest morgue for identification. Unfortunately none of the cadavers had hammertoes. But this did not stop the

33

interest in bodies; the reward of fifteen thousand was a ten-year salary in most cases. Mitchell was forced to make a number of trips to Montreal, New York, Buffalo and Chicago to view decomposed bodies. The publicity he received on his arrival in each city compensated for the odorous task.

Meanwhile, back in Toronto, Guthrie's detective force had been making some headway where none had been produced by Mitchell or Hammond. They checked into the Cycle Livery, next to the Grand Opera House, questioned salespeople at Lyon's Typewriters and William Curran's Hat Shop, asking each person—Do you know Mr. Small?—When did you last see Mr. Small?

Everyone along Adelaide Street knew Ambrose. Jack Dunlop, the florist across the road, saw him often but could not remember specific dates. At the Warden Hotel, on the west side of the Opera House, Ambrose was a familiar figure, especially in the company of Flynn, but memories had grown dim as to times and dates.

Harry Daily, restaurateur, knew Small by sight but had never spoken with him. Charles Reed in the candy shop knew both Small and Doughty but had not spoken to either of them, as contracts for candy-vending were given to one of Small's cronies. George Howarth was Small's barber. He had not seen him since late November, on the day before Small was to go to Montreal to talk with Trans-Canada Theatres. Howarth told detectives that Small was a skinflint and in the fifteen years he had been cutting his hair he never gave him a tip, although he did present him with a token gift at Christmas. Tobacconist Max Schlifer supplied Small with imported Havana cigars and wondered why his number one customer had dropped out of sight. No, he had not seen Small since November. At the Regent theatre, down the street from the Grand, the staff had not seen Small, though he and Theresa were the owners.

Doughty was the booking manager for this enterprise and he too had not been seen.

One of the detectives walked up to Ralph Savein, who sold newspapers at the corner of Adelaide and Yonge. Showing him the photograph of Ambrose Small, he asked, "Do you know this man?"

"Yes, sir, that's Mr. Small."

"Was he a customer of yours?"

"Yes, sir, he bought the New York Sunday Times every week, every Tuesday to be precise."

"And when did you last see Mr. Small?"

"On Tuesday night, December second," Savein replied, having recalled that date after reading of the disappearance.

The detective gulped. "What time did you see him?"

"At five-thirty o'clock."

"How can you be sure of the date and time?"

"Because Mr. Small couldn't wait to get the Times for the horse-race results and I would get it from the New York train which came in at five every night . . . and on Tuesday, sharp at five-thirty, Mr. Small would come over."

"How do you recall that particular date?" continued the detective.

"Because the Times had not arrived. Mr. Small was terribly angry. I had never heard him curse like that before. He stormed away in an ugly mood, I can tell you."

"And why was the Times not in?"

"There had been a snowstorm in New York and the trains were a day late. . . . The Times didn't come in until Wednesday."

"Did Mr. Small come Wednesday for his paper?"

"No, I never saw him again."

This information indicated that the lawyer Flock was not the last to see Small. It meant that Small must have left the

Opera House very soon after Flock's departure. Mitchell questioned Savein at considerable length but was mostly concerned with the direction Small had taken after the conversation about the *Times*. Savein said heavy snow was falling and he couldn't remember the direction, just the shadowy figure disappearing into the darkness.

Unfortunately Savein was wrong. Mitchell's department found that the *New York Sunday Times* had arrived on that Tuesday, December 2, on time. Savein, it was believed, had simply been looking for notoriety.

Mitchell talked to William Wampole, who operated the candy concession and Opera Glasses counter at the Grand. Wampole recalled that he had arrived at seven the night of December 2 and the only person he saw was manager James Cowan.

Cowan was interrogated for many hours by Hammond, and Cowan revealed that he believed "that was the night that I heard Doughty and Mr. Small arguing in the office." He said that was not unusual, but it did provide Hammond with the knowledge that Small was in the Opera House at curtain time. Cowan said he didn't listen to the argument beyond the office door as he had to hurry and raise the curtain at eight sharp for *Revelations of a Wife*. The House was packed that night.

"Did Mrs. Small come to the theatre that night?"

"No, Mr. Hammond, she did not, although she usually dropped in at curtain time . . . but that night she didn't come."

"Did you see Percy Small?"

"I may have seen him, but I can't recall."

"Who else would be working in the theatre that night besides Doughty, Small, Wampole and yourself?"

"Well, Ernie Reid would be there."

"What was his duty?"

"He was in charge of the vending machines, you know, chocolate bars, cigarettes and gum," said Cowan.

"Did you see him that night?"

"I can't recall. At eight I was backstage for some time, making sure everything went on schedule."

"Who else would be in the theatre?"

"The furnaceman, Thomas Shields."

"Was he there that night?"

"He would have to be, as he fired up the steam in the boilers, but I never saw him. In fact, I rarely ever saw him. He closed the theatre after midnight when he banked the furnace. The next morning he would clean up the aisles, and so on."

"What kind of a man is Shields?"

"Very old and hard of hearing . . . he must be in his late seventies . . . a little doddery."

"Who else that you recall came into the theatre that night?"

"I know Thomas Flynn was there, he often came in late at night to pick up Mr. Small and they would go out together, usually to Orpen's place to gamble."

"And Flynn was positively there that night?"

"Yes, he was upset by not seeing Mr. Small, and Doughty was not there either at that time."

"What time would that have been, Mr. Cowan?"

"I guess about ten-thirty."

"How can you fix the time?" pressed Hammond, wondering again why Mitchell hadn't interrogated the staff.

"Mrs. Small called me at eleven and asked if her husband was around. I said that I hadn't seen Mr. Small but that Thomas Flynn was pacing the lobby. She asked to speak to him and I heard him say, 'Why don't you leave him alone . . . he's just having some fun, I guess.' "

"What did Flynn do after that, if anything?"

"He went next door to the hotel to see Fred Lamb and buy a drink."

"I thought the hotel was closed."

"Not for friends of Mr. Lamb. He keeps a liquor supply in

his office and both Flynn and Mr. Small go in after theatre closing for a drink of whisky."

"Did you see Doughty leave the theatre that night to catch a train for Montreal?"

"No, I was backstage, mostly."

Hammond told Cowan he had been helpful in providing the details of that night as he saw and recalled them. As he was leaving Cowan, he turned and asked once again, "Did you see anyone else come into the lobby that night?"

"No sir, no one came through the front door, that is reasonably certain . . . no one during the time I was in the area."

Hammond pricked up his ears.

"Is there a back door?"

"Yes, although we were not supposed to know about it or discuss it. . . . Mr. Small's orders."

"Where does it lead to?"

"To Mr. Small's private room."

"Where is this private room?"

"It's hidden behind the curtains beyond the front office."

"Have you ever seen it?"

"No."

"What was it used for?"

"Mr. Small's private affairs . . . even Theresa didn't know about it."

"Well, well. Who has the keys for this office? I'd like to have a look at it."

"Only Mr. Small had the key but Jack Doughty might also have a key," explained Cowan.

"How did Small get into this office without being seen?" asked Hammond.

"It was connected by a secret stairway to Theatre Lane, at the side, and Mr. Small entered the place by the side stairway whenever he didn't want to be seen."

"And why didn't he want to be seen?"

"I've heard he had girlfriends in there at night."

"Was the office soundproof?"

"I sometimes heard distant sounds, but indistinct . . . yes I would say almost soundproof."

"Did the furnaceman, Shields, know of this office?"

"I doubt it. He was mostly in the basement and worked in the body of the theatre."

"Doughty knew of it?"

"Of course, it's next to his office, which is the main theatre office."

"Did Theresa know of it?"

"Heavens, no, not that I know of. She did a lot of snooping, but the office was well hidden."

"Did Percy Small know of it?"

"I don't know, I never heard him mention it. . . . It was the boss's hide-away."

"Did Thomas Flynn know about it?"

"I doubt it and I think if he knew he would have asked about it, especially the night that Mr. Small was missing and he was looking for him."

Next, Inspector Hammond called Guthrie and Mitchell and asked them to meet him immediately at the Opera House. When they arrived, he told them of the secret room at the rear of the main office and the detectives at once found a formidable oaken door behind the thick burgundy curtains on the south wall. They could not find a key anywhere in the office and a locksmith who was rushed to the theatre revealed that the door was bolted from the inside.

"Let's try the side door," suggested Hammond. The officers could find only one doorway off the lane at the east side of the theatre. It was a heavy windowless door, and it was unvarnished, giving the impression that it had not recently been used, if ever. Unable to force the lock, two constables battered it down and the detectives walked slowly in single file up the narrow musty stairway toward the front of the theatre. There were no electric light fixtures of any kind and Hammond, with the narrow walls pressing on his shoulders, squeezed his way slowly along behind the glow of his flashlight.

A door barred the way, and the detectives were forced to retreat outside while this barrier was broken down. They returned up the stairs and walked into an unlighted room. A switch was located by flashlight near the passage doorway and the soft glow from a crystal chandelier revealed an opulent retreat, small in dimension but adequate for Ambrose's purposes.

The walls were hung from ceiling to floor with heavy and obviously expensive drapes, thick and luxurious enough to contain normal sounds within the narrow room. The rug that covered the floor from wall to wall was thick and luxurious too, and Hammond marked in his notebook that it was an Oriental. A mahogany bar was attached to one of the walls, next to the outside door. A large nude painting graced the wall on the other side, which was next to the theatre office.

Along the wall on the street side of the room was a magnificent bed, deep and buoyant, with satin sheets and satin pillows shimmering in the subdued light. The bed appeared to have been used; the sheets had been tossed in a haphazard manner to the foot of the mattress. A musty smell pervaded the room; Hammond thought it might have been caused by stale cigar smoke. There were no windows, and only two doors were located, one to the inner office of the theatre and the other to the outside.

Detectives noticed an open bottle of rye whisky on the bar. There were two glasses, one of which was stained dark brown, indicating that an unfinished drink had evaporated and contributed to the smell of the boudoir.

The utter silence of the room—which reminded Hammond of an Egyptian tomb—the gathering of dust on the bar and on the headboard of the opulent bed, gave the detectives the feeling they had entered another world, a place where no person belonged except Ambrose Small and his private loves.

They listened to ascertain if sounds could enter the retreat either from inside the theatre or from outside. But all was silent. They found that the huge oaken door behind the curtains was closed by a number of steel spikes so that it could never be opened from the theatre side.

There were no papers in the room, no clothing of any kind, no washroom facilities, only a porcelain chamber pot beneath the bed. It was stained. There was not a single clue as to when the boudoir had last been used or by whom. The bar was well stocked with whisky and wine, and held also a container of perfume. The fine crystal glasses neatly ranged in the bar shelves were gathering dust but obviously had been clean when placed there, and Hammond expressed the opinion that Small might have employed a maid.

"I would sure like to find her," he said.

"What makes you think it was a woman?" asked Guthrie.

"It might have been a man, a confidant of Small's. This bloody case gets deeper every minute."

"Let's have a chat with Clara Smith," suggested Inspector Hammond. "She may provide all the answers we require at the moment."

"A good idea," replied Mitchell. "This place gives me the creeps. There's something about it that makes me shudder."

Chapter Four

Clara Smith was a vivacious brunette with an infectious smile and a way of walking that would stir the sensual desires of any male. She was a pretty girl, perhaps not over thirty, with a quick lilting laugh, and a sharp retort ready for any searching question. She greeted Hammond and Mitchell with a curtsy and the detectives were delighted with her fine manners. They told her they were concerned with the disappearance of Small and the possibility of foul play. Clara Smith agreed.

"Amby would never have forsaken me," she pouted. "Why, I knew him better than his own wife did. She was never responsive to his charms. And my Amby had many charms."

"Yes, yes," coughed Hammond. "But where could he be? What has happened to him? . . . Do you know where he is?"

"Someone must have done him in," she said. "Amby would never have gone away without telling me. He loved me."

She had not seen him, she said, since the night of December 1, when they had dinner together at the Walker House Hotel. He was to have called her the next day but failed to do so, and she had not heard from him since.

Had Miss Smith tasted the delights of the secret boudoir in the Opera House?

She had not. Her apartment was their trysting place.

Was she surprised to learn that Small had a private room with a secret entrance?

She was not surprised. She had known that Amby had dallied with members of the chorus line and had squired many young women since he started his theatres, but she was adamant that he had had no such involvements since meeting her, more than a year before his disappearance.

When asked by Mitchell if she was the "designing woman" that Theresa Small had referred to when first questioned about her husband's disappearance, Clara Smith replied quickly: "I hope so."

Had she ever met Theresa Small?

Never.

Did she know John Doughty?

Yes, very well; she considered Doughty a chronic "beefer" and she considered the threats he had made against Ambrose were more jocular than serious.

Did she know any names, any specific persons who were enemies of Small's?

No. She knew only what Ambrose told her and that was that he had many enemies, particularly gamblers whom he had "destroyed" at the gaming tables.

Clara Smith ended her remarks by saying that Theresa was the business partner and she was the love partner and that was that.

Hammond and Mitchell were impressed with Clara Smith. She appeared to speak honestly and her bouts of laughter could not conceal that she was deeply worried over her benefactor's disappearance. Her affection for Small seemed genuine and had developed since the first time she had met him while attending the Woodbine Race Track with Thomas Flynn, whom she had met at a business party.

Missing from the interrogation was the question of why and how often Clara Smith wrote love letters to Ambrose and what was the purpose of letters when the two were within telephone distance each day and often spent afternoons and evenings together. Mitchell at this period of the investigation was un-aware that Theresa Small was in possession of one of Clara Smith's letters, which had mysteriously come into her posses-sion several weeks before her husband's disappearance. Had Mitchell known of the letter, he might have been able to question Miss Smith as to its contents and determine if they could have been the basis of a separation of the Smalls or for the disappearance or even the murder of Ambrose.

After Clara, Hammond and Mitchell had three further persons to interrogate, first of whom was Thomas Shields, the furnaceman at the Opera House. During the past three months, Shields had been seriously ill and could not be ques-tioned. Now, his health had improved.

He revealed a sinister tale. He recalled watching Doughty and Small fighting one another in the furnace room and Doughty was holding a shovel over Small's head. Shields was horrified. Badly frightened, he had hurried from the fur-nace room and gone home, not telling anyone what he had seen.

"What night was that?" asked Mitchell.

"The night of December 2," replied Shields.

"How do you recall the precise date?"

"I became very ill that night, right after what I had seen, and I would never forget the date after that."

"You knew that we were trying to solve Mr. Small's disap-pearance; why didn't you come forward with what you've just told us?"

"I am old and I was afraid."

"You're positive you saw Doughty fighting with Small, but was there anyone else in the furnace room during this fight?"

Shields replied slowly through a spasm of coughing that he could not be certain. He had peeked through the crack of the furnace-room door when he heard the fight and he watched for only a few seconds before scurrying away. At this point it became obvious to the officers that Shields was in no condition to talk further, as his emotions were intensifying his medical problems.

Next to be questioned was Fred Osborne, a former janitor of the Opera House. He said that he had quit his job after a verbal battle with John Doughty. His memory was poor when it came to recalling the behaviour of Small and Doughty when they were seen together, but Osborne was quite positive in his statement that Doughty hated Small and often spoke of his plans to murder Small and run away with the theatre money. Osborne said he became so tired of Doughty and his "hare-brained" criminal schemes that eventually he had a showdown with him and stalked from his job. That was in 1918. He had not seen Doughty nor Small since that time.

After leaving Osborne, the two detectives drove to the Opera House en route to Court Street Police Station. There was something on Hammond's mind and he wanted to talk to Cowan again to ascertain whether or not he had heard anything new around the theatre that might help the investigation. Cowan had not heard anything new since he had accompanied the officers during the search of the Small's private room. However, he had been thinking things over and recalled that on December 3, the day after Small's disappearance, Theresa came to the Opera House and spent some time rummaging through the office. She appeared to be looking for some particular object but what it was, he didn't know.

"Maybe she was looking for the secret key," laughed Hammond.

"Oh, I doubt it," replied Cowan. "I am pretty positive Mrs. Small knew nothing of the private room, unless of course Doughty told her about it."

"Why would Doughty reveal his boss's secret?" pressed Hammond.

"I think Jack could be capable of anything if he was mad

enough, and he was sure angry about the sale of the theatres."

"You think he might take revenge on Ambrose by telling his wife about the secret room?"

"He might. Jack would do crazy things sometimes."

"But Theresa was party to the negotiations; she would be as blamable as Small."

"I guess so."

Hammond thanked Cowan for his further assistance and he thought it interesting that Theresa had come to the theatre to look for something. He would have to learn what that something was, when the time came to interrogate Mrs. Small.

Next on the list was Alderman Alfred McGuire, a member of the Toronto City Council and Small's insurance agent. He corroborated the Cowan story that Theresa Small came to the Opera House on December 3. He saw her enter and leave and she was in the theatre for "a half an hour or more."

At this period in the investigation, Inspector Hammond thought it was time to "have a talk" with Theresa Small, but Mitchell and Guthrie would have none of it. They agreed, and they were supported by police chief Harold J. Grasett, that all clues at the moment pointed to John Doughty. His threats against Small, his seeking the assistance of others to help him harm Small, his fight in the furnace room on the night of Small's disappearance, were all tight-fitting evidence that Doughty had a pathological hatred of Small and might have been capable of killing him. But none of this involved Theresa, so why bother her in her time of grief?

Hammond blew up. He stalked from the police station and drove to Queen's Park, the headquarters of the Ontario Provincial Police. He told Victor Williams, the Commissioner of the O.P.P., that he had enough evidence to lay a murder charge against John Doughty. But Williams told Hammond to cool down. There was no body, and a murder charge could not be laid at that time in Canada unless there was a body, with evidence of murder on the body.

Williams also reminded Hammond that the Small case was Toronto's case and that his department was only assisting the investigation. Austin Mitchell was in charge, and that was that.

Mitchell and Hammond rarely spoke to each other after this time. There was a move to replace Hammond by Inspector William Lougheed but Hammond complained bitterly that he had worked hard on the case and resented being replaced merely because Guthrie and Mitchell were overly protective to Theresa Small. He attributed this to the fact that the two officers were "afraid" to question her when there was little evidence to link her with the disappearance. Hammond believed that Theresa could fill in the gaps.

It was now July 1920, and around this time also the R.C.M.P. issued Wanted bulletins on John Doughty, distributing photos and description to all parts of Canada, the United States, Great Britain, and France, and to police departments in the far-flung corners of the Empire.

In Toronto, Alfred Elson, a Toronto caretaker, arrived at police headquarters with some information he thought Mitchell should know. He recalled that on the night of December 2, he was walking home not more than four blocks from Small's Glen Road home when he heard voices coming from the darkness down in the ravine. Moving quietly through the underbrush he came upon four men who were burying something in the frozen ground.

This was the kind of information that Mitchell was looking for. Within minutes, he was on his way northward to the Rosedale ravine with a squad of constables close behind him. Newsmen were quickly on the scene and digging continued through the day without result. Elson was never quite sure where he had seen the four men in the ravine, being dark and all.

Next, Mitchell received a "confidential" from the New York City Police Department. A telegram sent from Niagara Falls, New York, to a shady figure in Manhattan, whose name was not revealed, was intercepted by police after a tip from a Western Union Telegraph office.

"Hold Small until tomorrow morning," it read. "Don't let him go under any circumstances."

It was signed S. H.—Niagara Falls.

The telegram had not yet been delivered and New York detectives in touch with Mitchell by telephone said that a massive raid would be immediately planned as both the name of the person to whom the wire was addressed and the address itself, were genuine.

The intercepted message seemed promising and Mitchell waited for the result of the raid.

The man to whom the wire was addressed swore he never heard of Small and had no friends in Niagara Falls. "Someone is trying to pin a rap on me," he protested, and the New York police, after several days of investigation, decided the whole thing was a hoax. From a noted attorney in New York City, Mitchell next received a number of cables. This attorney had helped Jesse and Frank James at their last trial. He told Mitchell he had received a number of letters from someone called "B. B. Friend" who, he presumed, had underworld connections. This "B. B. Friend" stated that Small was being held by gangsters for ransom and that negotiations for his release would be started in the next few weeks.

Nothing happened. New York police said the letters were genuine but the whole affair could be a hoax. Besides, the Jameses' attorney was now senile and looking for publicity.

At this time, Sir Arthur Conan Doyle, creator of Sherlock Holmes, arrived in New York and was immediately questioned by reporters of the *World Telegram*. The first question was what he thought of the Ambrose Small disappearance up in Toronto.

"A very interesting case," mused Sir Arthur.

"Would you lend your talents to the case?"

"By Jove, I might if I was asked, but no one has approached me on the matter."

This prompted headlines in Toronto and New York: SHERLOCK HOLMES MAY ENTER SMALL MYSTERY.

In Chicago, a headline blazed across the top of the *Tribune*: WORLD'S GREATEST DETECTIVE TO SOLVE SMALL CASE.

In Los Angeles a banner line in bold front-page type screamed: SHERLOCK HOLMES TO REVEAL TORONTO MYSTERY.

All this made stirring news copy but Austin Mitchell decided no one but himself was going to solve this case. And Sir Arthur Conan Doyle was never invited to discuss the matter.

Mitchell was now approached by a spiritualist whose reputation was well-documented. He informed the detective that Small's Astral Body had been seen floating through the air—a sure sign in the occult world that Small was dead. Mitchell gave this announcement to the press. A mind-reader informed Mitchell that Small was buried in the city dump. On this assertion, Mitchell ordered a squad of police to take a steam shovel from the Department of Works and tear up the Toronto dumpyard. This took several weeks and nothing was found. Mitchell's advertisements in magazines and newspapers brought thousands of letters from cryptographers, crystal-ball experts and occult scientists from all parts of the world, and he perused every letter with infinite care.

While immersed in this extra-sensory analysis, Mitchell was approached by George Soucy, an engineer with the Mac-lean Publishing Company of Toronto. Soucy had been reluctant to approach Mitchell earlier, because he thought that his fellow employees would make fun of him. But his recurring nightmares drove him to police headquarters.

He swore that on the night of December 2, very late, he saw Small in a black automobile speeding north on Yonge Street. Small had tried to get a message to him but was restrained by a number of men.

By this time, Mitchell had received so many varying reports on Small that he was ready to throw up his hands. He merely noted Soucy's statement in the register in the detective office and went about his own work. Fred Lennon, sales manager of Canadian Universal Films Ltd., told Mitchell that Doughty was a "bad actor" and had mentioned to him on six occasions over two years that he had plans to kidnap Small.

"Doughty hated Small with all the passion at his command," said Lennon. "He was always dreaming up ways to get rid of Mr. Small. He was crazy, downright nuts. Small used to laugh at him and would tell Doughty to drop dead."

Mitchell talked with Lennon for an entire day, trying to trace the habits of Doughty. He confided to Lennon that he was beginning to have second thoughts about the fight in the furnace room at the Grand; it was just possible that Doughty had killed Small that night and heaved the body into the flames of the furnace.

Checking with Toronto forensic experts, Mitchell learned that the heat of the steam furnace would consume most of a human body but might leave a skull reasonably intact if it was banked shortly afterwards and the ashes emptied the next morning.

Where did the furnace ashes of the Grand disappear after they had been dumped in the alleyway at the rear of the theatre? The Toronto Refuse Department had the answer. In the week of December 2, the ashes would either have been dumped into Rosedale Ravine, on its east side, or onto the frozen surface of Toronto Bay.

Mitchell and a squad of men raced to the bay. The ice had melted and the ashes had sunk to the bottom. He called for a dredge. At Rosedale dump, where so much digging had occurred earlier, Mitchell directed steam shovels to the great piles of ashes, an area that had previously been overlooked.

Meanwhile, Hammond and his provincial officers were gathering material on the Smalls, the Doughtys, and Theresa's family, the Kormanns.

Jeannie, the sister of John Doughty, was next on the investigation list. She was a comely woman with a finely etched face, cornflower-blue eyes and light brown hair, naturally curly, with small ringlets dancing across her brow. She was petite in figure and appeared to glide when she walked. She had an engaging smile and likable personality, bright and vivacious. She had been in love with her brother John and she never married.

Born in Toronto in 1874, she was three years older than John and from the time he was born, Jeannie fondled and cared for him, at first like a plaything and then as a mother, and later as his closest friend and confidant. She was the product of strict Scotch-born parents. Her father was born in Glasgow and her mother in Brechin and their marriage was performed in Glasgow just before they departed by boat for Canada.

When they arrived in the bustling city of Toronto, her father found a job as a shipping clerk and within a year the couple purchased a semi-detached brick house on River Street, a stone's throw from the exporting firm where Doughty was employed.

Five children were born of the union. Jeannie was the eldest. She was followed by William, then John. A son, James, died in infancy; then a daughter, Isa, was born. John, who was born in 1877, was the idol of Jeannie from the beginning. She walked him to school each day from their River Street home. She taught Sunday School and John was in the class. She taught him music. His life was her life, and in his late teens, when she found a job for him, she would be waiting for him at the corner each night as he alighted from a tram. In their spare time, Jeannie taught John bookkeeping, which paved the way for his future position as secretary at the Grand Opera House.

Doughty was twenty-seven when he was recommended to Ambrose Small. Investigation showed this employment started around 1904, soon after Small and his wife bought the Opera House. The association of the two men was close, and Doughty was helpful in the acquisition of other theatres for the growing Small chain. He was well paid for his services and received a substantial raise in 1909 when Ambrose learned that John was in love with a French-Canadian from Penetanguishene, Ontario.

On August 31st of that year, John Doughty and Berthe Marchildon were married in a Protestant church, with Berthe changing her religion to John's. This was a traumatic blow for the staunchly Roman Catholic Marchildon family, and the couple were continuously harassed by members of Berthe's family and the priests of their church. Investigators believed that, at this period in his life, John Doughty became embittered against the Catholic Church. The first child, John, arrived in June of 1910. Next, on October 1, 1911, twins were born, a boy George and a girl whom they never had the chance to name. She died of whooping cough a week after her birth. But the worst blow was to occur several days later. Berthe, weakened by the birth of twins, caught diphtheria and died without leaving the maternity ward.

John went back to Jeannie, who enthusiastically accepted the new position in his life as mother to his sons. She never relinquished this duty until the boys left home a score of years later.

When Mitchell and Guthrie arrived at 8 Kingsmount Road, where Jeannie had moved from River Street to be with her sister Isa Lovatt, they found her to be gracious and polite, and yet nervous, and there was no doubt in their minds that Jeannie was deeply disturbed over the disappearance of her brother.

She told them she had had no word from John, not even a card or a letter, nothing, since he left the city after the Christmas holidays.

"Your brother was back from Montreal at Christmas?" asked Mitchell.

"Yes he came back twice after starting work in Montreal on December 3."

"And what was the purpose of these visits?"

"He said he had some business affairs to clear up and I think they were about the Opera House and Mr. Small. He had also rented our old house on River Street and he had some rents to collect."

"Where else did he go? Who else did he see?"

"On both occasions he saw Mrs. Small."

"What?" gasped Guthrie. "He visited Theresa Small?"

"Oh yes, at her Glen Road home."

"Do you know the purpose of those visits?"

"No. John never brought his business to the house although I do know he was angry at being transferred to Montreal because of the theatre sale. He wanted most to be near his boys and I can't say I blame him."

"What did you say to that?"

"I told him Montreal wasn't that far away and he could be home every week-end."

"I understand the boys' mother passed away when they were babies?" Austin Mitchell remarked.

"Yes, I have taken care of them since then."

"And John has always remained at the family home during all those years to be with his sons?"

"Yes, except when he married again."

Both Guthrie and Mitchell leaned forward in their chairs and for a moment they were unable to collect their thoughts. It had never occurred to them that John Doughty might have a second wife, and they were well aware that it had never occurred to Inspector Hammond, either.

"A second wife," pondered Mitchell, out loud. Perhaps Doughty was with her now.

Guthrie was angry. Here was his department searching all over Canada and the United States for a man who had a wife, a wife whom no one knew about and who might be living right under their noses.

"Where is she?"

"I have no idea."

"Well, does she reside in Toronto, or where?"

"The last time I saw her she was living in Toronto, but I don't know where."

"When was the last time you saw her?"

"I only saw her once in my life, a few days after the marriage. Both Isa and myself forbade her to come to the house."

"Why?"

"We didn't like her, she seemed cheap and coarse."

"Tell us the story of this marriage," Guthrie asked Jeannie, "because I think we may be over some of the shock by now."

She then related in a soft voice, sometimes hesitantly as she searched her memory, the story of her brother and his later years with Ambrose Small. She said that John's problems with Ambrose were that he thought he wasn't paid enough and felt he should be given the chance to share in the profits of the organization he had helped to build.

She knew that John, sometime around 1915, was not getting along with Small; he became nervous and irritable and would lapse into long periods of sulkiness and lonely contemplation. He began to drink, and Jeannie was forced to reprimand him on many occasions over his deteriorating behaviour. In 1916—toward the end of that year, as well as she could recall—John came home less and less often at nights and she suspected that he might be "playing around" like his boss, yet it came as a shock to Jeannie and her sister when John showed up one day in 1917 with a woman on his arm.

He told them he had just married Connie Spears, a chorus girl, and they were off on a honeymoon. Small had given them a wedding gift and Jeannie believed it might have been money, despite the fact that John was always referring to Small as a "skinflint."

The marriage apparently got away to a bad start. Jeannie told John that Connie was not moving in to the house at River Street and the boys were to remain with her. The couple began to quarrel and from time to time John would come back to River Street alone. One night in 1918 he said that Connie Spears had left him, would not return to him, and he couldn't care less.

"Was it a legal marriage?" asked Mitchell.

"Oh, yes, I checked it out," she replied. "They were married in Toronto in a Protestant chapel some place or other."

"As far as you are aware, did your brother ever see her again, or ever hear from her again after 1918?"

"He said not."

"What happened to her?"

"He said she deserted him, ran away."

"Where would she go?"

"I don't know and don't care. My brother had no business marrying her."

"How did your brother meet this Connie Spears?"

"Mr. Small introduced them, she was one of his girls," replied Jeannie, and there was an unmistakable sneer in her voice.

"When you and your sister refused to permit your brother's bride to visit or live in his own house, how did he take it?"

"Very badly, he felt cut off from the world."

"You must have worried about him?"

"Oh, we did, but he had to learn a lesson."

"What was that?"

"Connie Spears was no woman for him."

Guthrie was about to ask Jeannie if she was jealous of this marriage but thought better of it, and he and Mitchell returned to headquarters to put out a Wanted bulletin on Connie Spears.

No trace of her was ever found.

The marriage certificate was discovered and the act of marriage was listed in the records but there was no record of another marriage or of death.

Connie Spears had disappeared from the face of the earth, just like Ambrose and Doughty.

Chapter Five

Theresa Small was a paragon of virtue, perched high on Toronto's social ladder. She was a woman dedicated to the premise that Canada should be one country under one throne but not under one religion. The Catholic Church believed her to be Heaven-inspired and a protector of the faith. She was a lavish benefactress of a number of Catholic orphanages and convents. Charming and intelligent, a collector of rare art and a musician of great talent, with an ability to speak eight languages, Theresa was also a shrewd businesswoman with an almost uncanny knowledge of marketing, stock manipulation and salesmanship.

To her family and friends she was a woman of graciousness. To the Orange Lodge of Toronto, she was a "beast in Angel's clothing" who had dedicated her life to the overthrow of Protestantism in Toronto. To her political friends and her many legal associates, she was a woman with an unblemished character. There were others who believed that Theresa was clever and sinister enough to plan the death of her husband at the moment when he could have involved her in a critical family scandal.

Detective Austin Mitchell and Inspector Hammond believed in her innocence. Yet they must have had doubts from time to time, as when she steadfastly refused to reveal the reasons for John Doughty's two visits to the Glen Road home in late December 1919. On another occasion, according to police files, Theresa begged Mitchell and Hammond not to question Percy Small, as he was "very nervous" and had "nothing to add to the evidence."

The investigation of her past revealed a life of culture and luxury in Canada and on the Continent. Her legal association with Ambrose showed a dedication to acquiring business enterprises and making money. While Ambrose was establishing a character linked to shady deals and criminal practices in gambling and liquor-running, Theresa was becoming prominent in the financial and social circles that dominated the city.

Contrary to some newspaper reports of the period and subsequent magazine articles on the Small case, Ambrose and Theresa did not acquire their millions along the "Horatio Alger" pathway. Theresa was rich when Amby married her.

Theresa met Ambrose Small as a result of a chain of events in the beer business. She was a Kormann and the Kormanns operated one of the largest breweries in Toronto, producing a slightly bitter-tasting beer which was attractive to the large English population. The secret was brought to Canada by Ignatius Kormann around 1860 when he immigrated from Alsace, abandoning the original family brewery.

Little is known of her early life in Toronto and in Europe. She was born in 1872, which would make her nine years younger than the man she would some day marry. She was educated in Toronto private schools and colleges and attended finishing schools in Paris and in Rome.

Unravelling the interrelationships of the Kormanns and the Smalls took some considerable investigation by the provincial detectives under Inspector Hammond. They were forced to start with the arrival in Canada of the Small and Kormann families.

Daniel Small was born in 1844 in a rough-hewn cabin in

Adjala Township, some fifty miles northwest of Toronto. His father and mother had immigrated to that part of Ontario during the early days of the Irish potato famine, about 1842. Many other Irish families came to Canada at the same time and settled on farms scattered over the flatlands and hills midway between Georgian Bay and Lake Ontario. Hardship was the Irish lot. The land of Adjala Township was heavy clay mixed with gravel and patches of swamp, and often covered with thick bush. For an Irish family, able to nurture the soil and raise crops on two or three acres with consistent rainfall and long summers, the transition to Ontario was hard and bitter. The summers were often drought-attended, the winters long and harsh; managing fifty acres was an impossible dream, and Daniel Small vowed to shake the soil from his feet and start life anew in the big city.

When he was just eighteen years of age, Daniel had married Ellen Brazil, a local farm girl, and their first child was Ambrose, born in 1863 in the same rough-hewn cabin in which his father had first seen the light of day. The birth incapacitated Ellen for many months, and she never fully regained her health. Daniel had a brother, Phillip, living in another cabin on the farm, and to him he left the fifty acres and some cattle and chickens, but he sold his farm equipment in nearby Alliston as he needed money to establish himself in Toronto. It was not with any regret that he and Ellen said farewell to the Adjala acres sometime during the late summer of 1876. Ambrose was then thirteen.

The trio arrived in the big city by train from the village of Tottenham. The sale of the farm implements and several head of cattle gave them a starting sum of slightly more than five hundred dollars. The family took living quarters on Church Street in downtown Toronto, in an area close to shopping, churches and schools. Somewhere along the route of these early years, Daniel became a Protestant or, at least, he brought young Ambrose up as a Protestant, the reason never being revealed.

Daniel got a job as a shipper at the Kormann Breweries on Duchess Street, only three blocks from his rooming house. The brewery was to the rear of the Kormann House Hotel, a popular downtown watering place. He was a likable fellow, and his ability to produce expeditious results in shipping and cut a wide swath in making friends caught the eye of Ignatius Kormann, president of the brewery. Daniel was elevated to salesman covering the hotels in Toronto.

The city was bulging with trade and immigration. There were more than 100,000 residents, of whom some 15,000 were children. Bounded on the west by Dufferin Street, on the east by the Don River, on the north by Bloor and on the south by Toronto Bay and Lake Ontario, the expanding city was bustling with all the spice and illicitness of a western frontier town.

Hundreds of prostitutes plied their trade along downtown streets as well as on the lonely pathways of High Park to the west of the city. An English trade official remarked in that year that more prostitutes were conducting business in Toronto than in any other city of its size in the world. Street corners, someday to be dominated by banks, sported hotels, some good, some bad, but all of them busy pouring beer and liquor into happy masses of people, mostly English, with a smattering of Scotch and a few Irish.

Front Street, running east and west along the shoreline of Toronto Bay, was the main thoroughfare. The Queen's Hotel, facing the busy waterfront, dominated the north central section of the street. Lesser hotels stood along the south side of Front, and to the east, where the steam of the breweries etched the skies, many small industries clung together along with row upon row of trading shops, wholesale houses, banks and insurance offices. To the west of Bay Street were collections of freight sheds and factories.

North of this activity, of noise and dirt from locomotives and lake steamers, retail shops blended into residential areas of attached red-brick tenements. Beyond this, the land rose and became a wilderness of hills and ravines known as Rosedale.

To Daniel and Ellen, Toronto was the most exciting place in all the world. Within a few minutes' walk of their rooms, they could reach the General Store of Timothy Eaton, at the northwest corner of Queen and Yonge streets, and the Robert Simpson store, across the road on the southwest corner. Hotels, more retail shops, theatres and livery stables were freely mixed and shared both sides of Yonge Street from the waterfront to as far north as Bloor Street where the cobblestones ended and the clay road began, winding down into the wildness of a tree-filled ravine and then upward to the hills that protected the city from the winter winds.

From Bloor Street northward on the rutted surface of Yonge Street, the toll gates were in operation. Daniel recalled that on a single trip to Adjala Township to visit his brother Phillip, he was forced to pay six tolls for the fifty-five mile distance.

The ambition of Daniel and other newcomers to Toronto was to live, some day, in the rich district that lay immediately south of the ravine that ran from east to west just north of Bloor. Sherbourne and Jarvis streets revealed the homes of the wealthy, great piles of red brick and stone with huge well-tended lawns and gardens and rows of magnificent trees.

In 1878, Toronto, though mighty in industry, trade and finance, was highly vulnerable in one respect.

Great masses of green and ripened hay lay piled on the city streets. Mountains of baled straw reared upward from the yards of livery stables. Thousands of homes were constructed

61

of pine. Many large buildings, including hotels, were created of oak and pine with coverings of plaster and cedar shingles with rock facings for decoration. Sawdust was spread on the streets to sop up mud and water. All of this was an invitation to disaster. The great Chicago fire had taught few lessons.

The first warning came in 1878 when the Grand Opera House burned to the ground and carried away several business places with it. When the theatre was rebuilt, a hotel was also constructed next door and, because of his knowledge of the beer business, Daniel was given the opportunity to operate the bar. There is some evidence that the Kormann family held the mortgage on this hotel, called the Warden, and Joseph Kormann, manager of the brewery, assisted Daniel in running the suds palace. By 1882, the hotel was flourishing. Daniel was operating the entire enterprise, rooms, restaurant and tap room, when Ambrose was first introduced to daily work—washing dishes in the bar. The Smalls were a busy and happy group. A daughter Florence had been born to Daniel and Ellen in 1879 and a second daughter arrived in 1884. Her name was Gertrude.

But Ellen's health, never robust, had been overtaxed, and soon afterwards she died. She was buried a Catholic in Toronto's St. Michael's Cemetery. Her death left Daniel to raise the three children and it placed a severe burden on Ambrose, who was forced by these circumstances to care for his two sisters during the daytime hours; at nights he worked at his father's bar, washing glasses and sometimes assisting in serving drinks. It was not long before he began to search elsewhere for a better job.

Daniel's association with the Kormanns grew into a bond when he began escorting Josephine Kormann, much to the concern of her mother, Mary Eva. But when Daniel proposed to Josephine and promised to turn to Catholicism, Mary Eva gave her consent, and she expected that Ambrose, Florence and Gertrude would automatically follow their father into the true church. They were married in 1885 and Daniel at forty-one was Josephine's senior by twenty-two years. In fact, Josephine was three years younger than Ambrose and six years older than Theresa.

But if Daniel turned Catholic, the children did not, and Daniel fought stubbornly to keep Ellen's youngsters solidly Protestant. It may have been that Daniel was more concerned over the future of Ambrose in a city that favoured Protestants, members of the Loyal Orange Lodge, and the Sons of England. He knew that the presence of Ambrose behind the bar had helped swell his business among the gentlemen of the financial district who were, almost to the man, Church of England.

Ambrose was now sporting a walrus mustache, managing the bar operations, watchdogging a booking operation in the rear of the hotel and working in the Grand at nights as a spare-time usher. It wasn't long before he was offered the position of assistant manager at the Grand and within a year he was Booking Manager, signing such hits as *School for Scandal*, a spicy melodrama, *Bertha the Sewing-Machine Girl* and many famous plays of the latter part of the last century. Daniel opened a liquor store at 54 Elizabeth Street, a seedy district in downtown Toronto. Ambrose was making money at the local race track because of his association with Racing Commissioner Flynn and with the gambling czar, Abe Orpen. Florence and Gertrude were in private schools. Josephine within the next five years produced two children for Daniel, Percy and Madeline.

By 1892, Ambrose at twenty-nine was a confirmed bachelor dedicated to making money. He already held mortgages in two Toronto downtown theatres while trying repeatedly to buy the Grand Opera House. The Grand was not for sale but Ambrose vowed to have it some day. Two or three years later, he had gained an international reputation as a "high-stakes" gambler and on at least one Woodbine race he "cleaned up" ten thousand dollars. The race was said to have been fixed, and Small was suspected among the gambling crowd of the city of being a race-fixer. His crony Flynn was keeping discreetly in the background, while Ambrose was building around himself an envelope of hate and distrust.

"You can call me anything, but don't call me Ambrose Small," growled a prominent Toronto racing enthusiast to exemplify the feelings of the track community. Small was now a member of the exclusive Toronto Yacht Club, the Empire Club of Toronto and the Canadian Club.

Ambrose also had a way with women. His stature was instantly forgotten when his blue eyes and his magnificent mustache ran head-on into the dancers of the chorus lines at the Opera House. Chorus girls were easy picking, he found. They were Americans, far away from home, craving good food, free booze and a big spender. Ambrose supplied all the necessary ingredients.

It did not seem possible to his friends that, with all the fun he was having, Ambrose would ever settle down to one woman and the straight life that was expected in the society of Victoria's Empire. But as the new century dawned, Ambrose met Theresa Kormann, the youngest of the Kormanns' eleven children, and the two began to share their Sunday walks along Bloor Street, though not the Sunday masses.

Mary Eva, matriarch of the brewery empire since the death of Ignatius, was well aware that Ambrose had been born into a Catholic family and had been raised a Protestant by the very man who, when he married her daughter Josephine, had himself rejoined the true church. She noticed that although Ambrose was stubborn in his beliefs, he nevertheless refused to discuss the Protestant faith, never attended a church, and was considerate and friendly with his Roman Catholic relatives and acquaintances.

To have Ambrose reintroduced into the Catholic Church, which in all probability would also attract the sisters Gertrude and Florence, would be for Mary Eva a religious victory unparalleled. But to rush Ambrose would be disastrous and she bided her time, inviting him often to Sunday dinners at the house. There is no doubt that Mary Eva could also see in the love affair the union of two family fortunes. But she did not live to see that wish come true. On October 15, 1902, she passed away at the age of sixty, leaving the brewery operations to her two eldest sons and an estate divided among sons and daughters.

Ambrose was not unaware of the legacy.

Although Mary Eva was under the turf at the side of Ignatius beneath an ornate red marble column in St. Michael's Cemetery, the children were, without exception, unyielding Catholics and Ambrose noted that Josephine, his stepmother and Theresa's sister, was to have a profound influence on Theresa's future decisions.

He acted promptly before a Catholic conspiracy could be used to tempt him into the fold. Six weeks after Mary Eva's death, Ambrose and Theresa were married quietly in Our Lady of Lourdes Catholic Church on Sherbourne Street. The couple travelled by train to New York City, stayed at the Waldorf, and attended the theatres and called on booking agents to make the honeymoon a dual success of love and business.

Persons who knew the Smalls at that time were convinced that Ambrose and Theresa were genuinely in love and it would seem that the strange combination of graciousness, culture and ultra-Catholicism with gambling, wenching, liquor-running and Protestantism could somehow survive and blossom.

There were those who believed that love was the catalyst. Some others, however, believed that Ambrose and Theresa were greedy for riches and had combined their talents and their private fortunes in order to become millionaires some day. Ambrose had also found the social status he longed for. To enhance this elevation, on his return from New York, he ordered architect's plans for the biggest and best home in Rosedale, as the ultimate wedding present to his bride. Theresa responded by pooling her savings with Ambrose and buying the mortgage of the Grand Opera House.

A promise was made between the two that Theresa could remain a Catholic with no interference whatsoever from Ambrose in her affairs with the Church, and Ambrose could remain a Protestant without any interference from her family. As far as Gertrude and Florence were concerned, it was apparently decided by the couple to let the girls follow the religion of their own choice.

This pact evidently had no ill effect on the close relationship between Theresa and her sister Josephine, and it may have been because Josephine could see the couple amassing a fortune and was assured by Theresa that her main goal in life would continue to be the supporting of Catholic charities, orphanages and convents.

During 1903 and 1904, the profits from the Grand Opera House and from the Regent Theatre, which Ambrose and Theresa had acquired, were booming. The couple began to look elsewhere for the possible expansion of their investments, other than in the stock market, which Theresa considered too risky. A frightening event in the spring of 1904 prompted them to diversify their financial holdings.

Theatre magnate, Ambrose J. Small, at his desk in Toronto's Grand Opera House.

Theresa Small was the leading benefactress of the Catholic Church in Toronto. She was a social leader, a linguist and an accomplished musician.

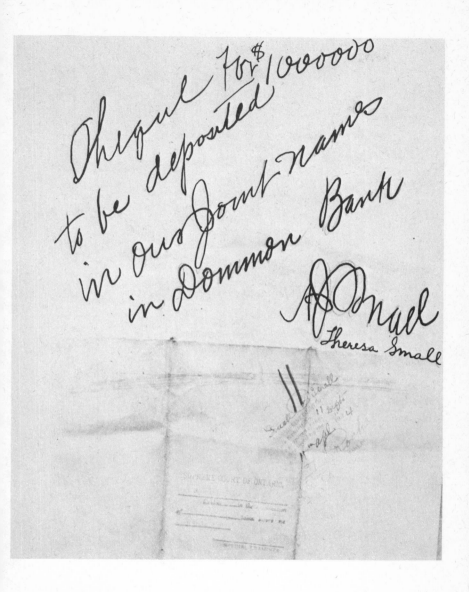

Ambrose and Theresa endorsed a cheque that made them
multi-millionaires that fateful December 2, 1919.

Toronto, Sept 6th
1903

This is the last will
and testament of Ambrose J Small
I devise and bequeath
all my real and personal
property whatsoever and whereso-
ever to my wife Theresa Small
and I appoint her my sole
administratrix & executrix

WITNESSES   Ambrose J Small
Mary Hormann
Madeline Holmes

Theresa Small had lost considerable weight in the 1930's when she was photographed with her attorney, W. N. Tilley.

This is the last Will of Ambrose Small, and although others were claimed to have been made, none was ever found.

The Small sisters, Gertrude and Florence, hated Theresa Small and vowed revenge.

John Doughty was the mystery man in the case. He had two wives and one disappeared.

The Smalls' maid, Catherine Dunn—seen here as she looked when she joined the Smalls and when she left them—would watch the mysterious carryings-on from behind the heavy curtains.

The Small home on Glen Road, in Rosedale, Toronto, as it was when the Smalls lived there. It stands to this day.

The Grand Opera House on Adelaide Street West in Toronto as it looked shortly after Small's disappearance.

THE WINDSOR HOTEL
MONTREAL

This man claimed that he was Ambrose Small but he did not possess Small's congenital secret.

In this letter from Montreal, of November 28, 1919, Small wrote that he had sold his theatres.

Ontario Racing Commissioner, Thomas Flynn, was the only person to inform police and the press that Small had vanished into thin air.

Theresa Small as she looked during the 1920's.

Small's girl friend was chubby Clara Smith.

Theresa Small found a number of letters from Clara Smith to Ambrose, letters that were deemed to be so filthy they could not be read in open court, and she placed them in her private black box where she kept her valuables and left the box wide open for Ambrose to find while she attended a musical concert on the night of April 2, 1918. Ambrose found the box and destroyed the letters and left the above note to Theresa.

2/4/

Theresa
Dear
Theresa

Dont bother Your

dear little head

about this rotten

stuff any more

It's all
over

And no earthly
use digging it
up any more.
You left the Black
Box will open
the night you went
to the Academy of Music
Musicale I saw it
and destroyed the whole
business to get it out of the
way and not bother either of us again Amb
(God Bless You)

The Rosedale Ravine was the scene of intense police searching.

A volunteer, one of thousands, digs for human bones in the Rosedale Ravine.

Human bones unearthed near Small's home were not his.

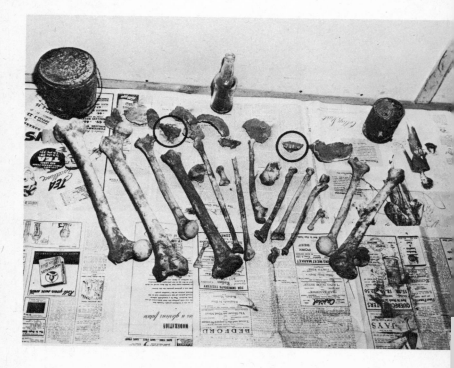

Chapter Six

On the blustery night of April 19, 1904, just a few hundred
yards from the Grand Opera House and the Regent Theatre,
the factory of E.S. Currie Tie Company, on Wellington Street,
just west of Bay, erupted into a ball of flame.

As dozens of female employees dashed from the smoke and
flame-filled structure, a tongue of fire shot up the elevator
chute and broke through a skylight to set fire to the pitch-
covered tar-paper roof, and within minutes the flames were
leaping high into the air and embers were carried over the
heart of the downtown area.

Two blocks north of the orange glow that marked the early
stages of this fire, police constable William Lennon was direct-
ing carriage traffic along Adelaide Street to the Grand Opera
House. The box office had opened and a small line of patrons
had gathered on the sidewalk. Then, a young woman, her eyes
dilated by fright, screamed at Lennon and pointed to the glow
of light. Lennon pulled the alarm lever on Box 12 at the corner
of Bay and Adelaide streets. In less than a minute, a horse-
drawn hose wagon and a steamer were rumbling south on Bay
from the Richmond Street Fire Station. Deputy Chief John
Noble saw fire leaping like angry waves across the alleyway
from the Currie Building and he knew at once he had a big one
on his hands. He turned in a second alarm.

Fire engines, pulled by heaving white horses with sparks

flying from their iron shoes, responded from Lombard and Portland Street Stations. The clang of firebells rang over the downtown district like harbingers of doom.

At the Grand, the curtain ran up for one of Small's most daring stage presentations, *Nellie the Beautiful Cloak Model*.

Fed by tinder-dry wooden window-frames and floor joists of seasoned lumber, the fire spread with overwhelming rapidity and Small closed the Opera House, asking the patrons to return the next night. The entire sky in the area of the theatre was a dull red glow and through this panorama of sinister colour spewed millions of firebrands that settled on tar-paper roofs, starting additional fires. Toronto was proud of its fire-fighting operations, with five steamers, one 65-foot water-tower wagon, one 85-foot aerial and ladder truck, five hook and ladders, two four-wheel chemical wagons and a number of extra hose and supply wagons.

But neither the men nor the equipment could face the holocaust that now surrounded them. In no time, the fire whipped by the freshening wind jumped across entire intersections of the downtown area and enveloped block after block of industry, office buildings, stables, hotels and transportation terminals. Freight sheds and old wooden wharves collapsed in huge showers of fire. Flames shot five hundred feet into the night sky and help began to arrive from as far away as Hamilton, Niagara Falls, Buffalo, and scores of other towns and cities within a hundred-mile radius of Toronto.

By mid-morning most of downtown Toronto was erased. Gaunt walls of seared brick and mortar, streets filled with rubble and wide hollow places where buildings once flourished, now lay silent but for the soft wind.

The Grand Opera House had been spared. So had the Regent Theatre.

"A miracle," Theresa told Ambrose.

"Goddamn lucky," Small told his friends over the bar next door, which had also survived the holocaust.

But whether it was luck or a miracle, both Ambrose and Theresa knew at that moment that placing almost all their personal fortune and theatrical earnings into a side-by-side venture when fire was an ever-present hazard could wipe them out at any time. This was foolish and dangerous. Toronto had lost 338 business firms with a loss of some ten and a half million dollars.

They decided to spread their investment. It was Ambrose who suggested that they buy up other theatres in the major cities of Ontario and then expand into the other provinces of Canada, to keep their profits moving into new investments. Theresa agreed.

Small could envision the day in the near future when from one single agency in Toronto, he and Theresa would control the vaudeville circuit into Canada by booking for all their own theatres, as well as for other theatres where there was no competition to their enterprises.

But first, Small needed a secretary-manager who would handle the paperwork of such an enterprise. Through an advertisement placed in the *Toronto World*, Small and Theresa met John Doughty. He was hired and Small, in his usual swift and nervous manner, bodily tossed the current manager into Adelaide Street with a farewell message: "Good riddance."

Detectives, delving into the business and personal lives of the couple, discovered that the association between Small and John Doughty had been turbulent right from the beginning and it was a good guess that the only reason Doughty was not fired was because he was producing. And Small liked production; personality traits he shoved aside like the ashes of his cigars.

Doughty was well paid and was the undercover agent assessing the profits and losses of theatres in which Small was interested. Doughty had a sharp eye for business and a sharper eye for padded accounts of receipts and profits and disbursements. From 1905 onward, the Smalls were able to quietly assess and then acquire theatres in London, Peterborough, Windsor and other cities.

But while the business team was working smoothly, the family tree was creaking at the roots. Florence and Gertrude were unhappy sisters. From time to time they read of the lavish spending of Theresa, her trips to Europe to buy paintings and sculptures, her visits to Rome, her travels to Paris. Of Ambrose, they knew he had acquired new theatres and was as prominent at Florida and Louisiana race tracks as he was at Toronto's Woodbine track. And since Ambrose had not increased their monthly living allowances since the marriage, they were bitter. One night they trapped their brother in the lobby of the Grand and demanded a larger allowance. The next night they openly insulted Theresa in the lobby and Ambrose had them ejected. They swore revenge against Theresa, blaming her for their problems.

Ambrose told Doughty to keep his sisters away from the theatre and to deliver their monthly cheques to them, personally. He also increased their allowances. Then he and Theresa and Doughty continued to move into other cities, acquiring further theatres and enterprises. But Doughty began to complain that he was doing all the work and the couple were making all the money. He, too, began to tell Small that he was underpaid, while Theresa was lavishing money on the Catholic Church, and he didn't think it was fair.

Small's answer to Doughty was almost always, "Don't bother me Jack, you never had it so good." And with Doughty fuming over his reports, the couple continued to reach toward their goal of a million dollars. They reached it about 1910 or 1911, police believe.

Then Theresa and Ambrose began to quarrel. Ambrose, though reluctant to break his earlier vows, was becoming tired of his Glen Road home being a haven for nuns and priests and he sarcastically referred to a shrine in the basement of the home as a hangout for hungry priests.

Theresa would have none of this criticism. The shrine was her private place of worship, her confession chamber, and beyond the eyes of Ambrose. By 1912, the childless couple were sleeping in separate bedrooms. Small was tiring of the marriage; investigators found that at about this period he began to travel to New York, Chicago, Denver and Florida, following the racing season or participating in wild parties with his cronies and chorus girls.

He was irritated also by Theresa's snoopiness. At one period, he could hardly start counting the money in the theatre office each night before Theresa was hovering over his shoulder. It was while she was on a trip to Rome for a private audience with the Pope that Small had construction crews reshape the rear area of his office. The secret office was installed, with a private stairway from the side lane. Doughty, it seems, agreed with this procedure, as he was never known to protest over the frequency of the parties held there.

It is doubtful that Theresa knew of this hidden retreat. Ambrose never returned to Glen Road before the small hours of the morning and Theresa's comments usually concerned his gambling at Orpen's. After her recurrent showdowns with Ambrose she would retire to her shrine in the basement, but they never allowed their squabbles or differences in religion to deter them from making more money. They were already in the millionaire class and Toronto society knew them as "those rich rich Smalls."

Daniel Small retired from the liquor business sometime in 1915, and within a few months the Kormanns disposed of their brewing interests and the Kormann House Hotel. With some of her share of the proceeds, Theresa built a Novitiate on Glen Road, almost directly across from the Small mansion. From this time onward, she devoted herself mainly to her religious institutions and her women's clubs, keeping close to her sister Josephine. But she had Ambrose place Percy Small, Josephine's son, in the Opera House as treasurer. Theresa wanted to know precisely what was being earned and what was being spent.

Small resented this intrusion and so did Doughty, who told Ambrose that he couldn't stand "the snivelling Percy," but Theresa wanted Percy employed in the business; she had an equal say with Ambrose, and Percy was hired. He was a quiet man with impeccable manners and a slight trace of snobbery in his precise articulation of words, which he had acquired at college. He disliked Doughty right from the start and it would appear, from the investigation, that he disliked Small also, but paid him reasonable respect because Ambrose was his uncle. Percy, it will be recalled, was also Ambrose's half-brother, since Daniel was the father of both of them. Small tolerated Percy and it may have been because he appreciated a little culture in the management and it could not be found in Doughty.

At about this time, detectives learned, Theresa had made a promise to the Catholic Church that she would will all her worldly belongings and money to the church, and that if she should predecease Ambrose half of all the estate would go to the church. Her husband's will, made in 1903 and unchanged throughout his life despite all rumours to the contrary, left all his wealth and possessions to Theresa with a proviso that the sum of $100,000 be set aside to earn interest which was to be paid to his sisters for as long as they lived.

This latter gesture was a balm to his conscience. He had promised when he was twenty-one that he would care for them all their lives, if need be, and it didn't appear that they would ever marry.

As the war years dawned, the Smalls had completed their acquisition of theatres across Canada and were travelling more often, but rarely together. Ambrose followed the racing season from Florida to California and Theresa, with Josephine, travelled to the Continent. On several occasions Theresa would join Ambrose in Miami for the racing season. She loved the social set more than she loved watching the horses.

She had gained weight with her lavish living, and by 1915 photographs showed her to be at least as heavy as Ambrose. She dressed in the latest fashion, ankle-length wool suits of beige in the spring and summer and sombre black suits and skirts with thick fur coats of black seal and other genuine furs in the fall and winter.

Theresa appeared less and less at the theatres and this may have been caused by a change in public demand, the need for lighter, bawdier and burlesque-type presentations to overcome the gloom of war. But although she appeared less at the Grand, she nevertheless kept her eye on the profits and disbursements which Percy brought to her, once weekly. Police believe that the mounting and open hostility between Doughty and Ambrose at this time must have been made known to Theresa, as Percy was the carrier of all news and business from the theatre to Theresa. And nothing ever escaped "little Percy" as Ambrose used to say.

Police had, by now, exhausted most of their research into the Small empire and were ready to interrogate the Kormanns. "Now's the time to talk to Theresa," snapped Inspector Guthrie.

Chapter Seven

Since the disappearance of her husband, Theresa Small had become a recluse, a woman who refused to see anyone connected with the investigation, with the exception of Austin Mitchell.

She would not answer the telephone nor would she speak to anyone unless the persons calling on the phone or at the house were members of the immediate family or priests and nuns of the Church. She no longer held weekly tea parties among her friends of the many women's associations to which she belonged.

Theresa had buried herself within the walls of her Glen Road mansion but was kept in touch with the business world by Percy Small who was assisting her with investments and the chores of bill-paying. When she left the house she was almost always accompanied by Josephine and these trips were mostly shopping visits to exclusive downtown clothing stores. Her custom of travelling to Europe during the winter months stopped in 1920, nor did she take her regular spring trip to Florida.

Theresa had closed herself off, even to the extent of having every mass and confession conducted at her basement shrine; abandoned were the weekly pilgrimages to Our Lady of Lourdes Church on Sherbourne Street, only a short walk away.

When she left the security of her home it was always in the rear seat of her Cadillac limousine and she would not even chance a walk to the Sisters of Service Convent a few hundred feet up the street and across the road from her home. She was nervous and frightened, and no wonder.

On Sundays, Glen Road never had so many gawkers and it was apparent why they were strolling through Rosedale. They would slow down in front of the Small mansion and often stop and loiter in the hope of catching sight of Theresa, only to be disappointed. When Theresa slipped out of the house, she waited until the chauffeur brought the car to the side door on the south side of the house and then with the rear door held open, she would slip inside quickly, draw the side curtains of the rear seat and be on her way, usually to her sister's.

News reporters and news photographers were the biggest pests at Glen Road. They would hammer on the front door while others would try the side and rear doors. But maids would always tell them "Mrs. Small is not at home."

Street-car tours into Rosedale were more crowded than usual, as the Small house was now on the list of famous homes. In fact, hundreds of visitors from all parts of Canada and the United States made it a point, while in Toronto, to see the place "where the millionaire lived."

Rumours had started that Small was dead and buried beneath the basement floor in the Glen Road house. These rumours increased the number of curious and on pleasant Sundays the street in front of the house was often crowded. It was necessary for the Toronto Police Department to keep a constable on duty at the residence on Sundays and discreetly near the house during the week. From time to time, detectives, mostly private sleuths, would join in the crowds, not only to watch for Theresa or visitors to the house but to mix with the curious and listen to the rumour of the streets.

Theresa hated all this. But she would not vacate the residence. It was close to the convent and to her closest friends, the nuns.

She was also hoping, some of her closest friends reported, that the intense news interest in Small's disappearance would wear thin. She was not to know that the interest would increase tremendously—in the case of certain newspapers, almost to the bounds of hysteria.

But it was quiet and lovely along Glen Road, that morning in the first week of July, 1920, when Mitchell and Guthrie arrived to "talk" with Theresa. Informed by a phone call from headquarters that they were coming, she was waiting for them when they arrived and greeted both detectives with a warm smile. Gracious and charming, she herself poured tea in the music room after one of the maids had brought in the sterling silver service.

No, she had heard absolutely nothing from Ambrose or his host of friends since his disappearance. Nothing. There had been no hint of kidnapping, no calls for ransom, just a great silence.

"Mrs. Small—just what do you think has happened to your husband?" asked Inspector Guthrie.

Without the least hesitation, Theresa replied: "I believe my Amby is in the hands of a designing woman, somewhere, and will come back."

"Have you any apprehension as to his health and his welfare?"

"Indeed, yes, but men of Amby's age do strange things —but they always come back."

"Would you consider me indiscreet if I asked if there is a possibility that Mr. Small might have had a . . . ah . . . a mistress?"

"It is just possible that he was spending a great deal of time with a woman called Clara Smith. . . . Here's a letter she wrote to him last November."

Theresa handed over a letter beginning "My Darling Amby," and signed, "your love forever, Clara." Both Mitchell and Guthrie read it and agreed it was a love-letter in every sense of the word. Instead of seizing the letter and keeping it on file in the Small Case, the officers returned it to Theresa and suggested she destroy it for fear its contents might somehow leak outside the house into the news columns.

Guthrie informed Theresa at this point, that although there was evidence that Clara Smith and Ambrose were well known to one another, Clara had not seen him since December 1, the night before his disappearance.

"She may be just waiting to go to him, somewhere out of the country," Theresa retorted, and Mitchell was sympathetic. But Guthrie thought that the length of time that Ambrose had made no contact with Clara, who was apparently his mistress, was an indication that if he ran away, he must have run away from both Theresa and Clara, and if there was a "designing woman" in the shadows, there was certainly no evidence of it.

Guthrie asked Theresa who had given her the letter, which was addressed to "Mr. Small" at the Grand Opera House. Theresa begged the officers not to ask her to reveal the source and they did not pursue the question.

"Have you ever seen or talked to Clara Smith?" asked Guthrie, who was conducting most of the interrogation.

"Miss Smith came here in January, I think, and she asked for me. I did not speak to her. Why should I speak to the woman who had stolen my husband?"

"Yes, yes," choked Guthrie, and steered the conversation in another direction. He told Theresa that there had been conversations with Jeannie Doughty and she had revealed that twice in December, John Doughty had come to Toronto to visit his family and on both occasions he said he was going to Glen Road to see Mrs. Small.

"Is this a fact?" asked Guthrie.

"Yes, Mr. Doughty came to see me about some business matters."

"What was the nature of the business?"

"It concerned some left-overs of the sale."

"Did you discuss your husband's disappearance?"

"I must refuse to discuss with you the private talks I had with Mr. Doughty on those occasions, they were personal and private and there were some business details. . . . This is most trying, and I ask your consideration."

"Of course, of course," blurted Mitchell.

"One more thing, Mrs. Small," continued Guthrie. "Have you seen John Doughty since those December meetings?"

"No."

"Have you heard from him, either by telephone or by letter?"

"No."

"Have you any explanation for his disappearance?"

"None, except that as far as I am concerned, John Doughty is a crazy man and you never know when he is going to say something or do something that appears to be caused by mental unbalance."

"Can you give us any examples?"

"Just ask any of the theatre staff, Mr. Guthrie. I cannot see the reason for all these questions. . . . I haven't seen Mr. Doughty and don't want to see him. Our business is over as far as he is concerned."

"Do you link Doughty with your husband's disappearance?"

"Not at all."

"There has been talk of amnesia. Did Mr. Small suffer from amnesia?"

"Not that I know of. . . . Amby was forgetful at times but he seemed to know what he was doing, after all he was a successful businessman."

"Finally, Mrs. Small, what do you really and truly think happened to your husband?"

Theresa thought for a moment and she was squeezing her lace handkerchief in her hands.

"Mr. Guthrie, I am convinced that Amby is somewhere in the hands of a designing woman."

"One more thing, Mrs. Small, did Doughty have rights to the missing bonds? Were they given to him, or had he permission to take them?"

"Mr. Doughty had no rights to those bonds. They belonged to my husband and myself and Ambrose would certainly not give them away—that is certain."

As the two officers left Glen Road and started back to headquarters, Guthrie asked Mitchell: "Well, what do you think?"

"I think Mrs. Small is a fine woman and has been badly shocked by all this. What do *you* think?"

"I had the feeling she was trying to pin Small's disappearance on Clara Smith—nothing concrete, mind you—just a feeling."

Chapter Eight

In the far-off cluster of lumber mills and unpainted shacks grandly known as Oregon City, about a dozen tortuous miles southeast of Portland, there resided a recluse and ne'er-do-well without formal or legal identification. He went only by the name of "Three Fingers." He was obviously well named as he had only three fingers on his right hand, thanks to an errant buzz-saw. Or so he said.

Oregon City was difficult to reach, yet it was a profitable place to work and live. Wages in the lumber and milling camps were the highest in the country. Labour was scarce and employers never asked questions of the thin working force that from time to time filtered through the forest and mountain wall. A man's background was his own business and that's exactly the way Three Fingers liked it.

Yet he was curious about the world beyond the mountains of Oregon. At least once a month he would shuffle into Portland and cautiously visit the main hallway of the state courthouse where the bulletins of wanted men were posted. Three Fingers would leaf through the circulars, first making sure there were no snooping police constables peering over his shoulders. After going through the entire lists, he would head back for the lumber camp, relieved.

During one of those periodic trips to Portland, sometime around the latter part of September 1920, Three Fingers paid his usual visit to the state courthouse and began to leaf through the bulletins. Suddenly his eyes popped open. The nerves at the nape of his neck tightened. Sweat began to form in the dirty creases of his brow. He looked around. No one was in sight. It was Saturday and the courtrooms were closed. Three Fingers liked Saturdays for that reason.

One of the Wanted posters had caught his attention, the one with the photograph. He removed the poster from the rest of the group, stuffed it into his lumberjack shirt and returned to Oregon City to study it. He was still shaking from the experience and the perspiration continued to flow from his forehead.

The more he studied the photograph and the information below it, the more he was convinced that the quarry was right there in Oregon City; in fact, living in the staff house next door. But he had to be careful. Accusing any man, rightly or wrongly, in a lumber camp wasn't the healthiest of occupations, he knew.

When Portland's chief of police Harry Fortune entered his office Monday morning, who should be waiting for him but Three Fingers. Fortune knew Three Fingers from away back and had long ago figured that the man was probably wanted for something back east.

"Whadya want?" snapped Fortune, shuffling through the overnight mail.

"There's a reward of fifteen grand on a bird from Canada, and I know where he is."

The Chief opened his eyes slightly and blew a cloud of smoke toward the brass fixture hanging from the ceiling. He was pondering. As a cop in Portland it would take ten years to earn that amount.

"Where is this bird?"

"Up the valley," replied Three Fingers cautiously.

"I'll go with you and we'll bring him in."

"No we won't," drawled Three Fingers, used to the ways of

police. "First, we make a fifty-fifty agreement on the reward, signed and witnessed before a notary, and then you'll have to go to work and double-check this guy. There's always a chance I could be wrong, but I don't think so."

The Chief and Three Fingers strode into an adjoining office where the court notary was located and between them agreed to split the police reward, if there was still a reward in effect. Then they drove to Oregon City, arriving at the lumber camps about an hour before closing time. The smell of pine sap stung the nostrils and soft blue smoke drifted over the campsite from the fires that were being kindled in the cookhouse. While Three Fingers stood guard at the staff house, Chief Fortune entered the room of a man known as Charlie Cooper in the camp but who resembled someone called John Doughty back in Toronto.

The room was sparsely furnished, having only a single cot, a dressing table with a small broken mirror over it, a chair, and a rough writing desk. There were no pictures on the walls and only a single arc lamp dangled from the ceiling. The smell of pine and cedar from the walls and ceiling was not unpleasant, the Chief thought.

A letter lay on the desk. It had been opened. It was addressed to Charles Cooper at the camp. The postmark was struck in Toronto, Canada. There was no signature and the contents of the finely written letter concerned the health of various unnamed people, referred to as "the little one" and "the bigger one" and "she" and "he" in an obvious attempt to avoid using names. But there was one line that provided a clue: "Jeannie is fine," it said.

Why mention only one person, he wondered. She must be very important in this guy Cooper's life. He placed the letter back on the desk and then after telling Three Fingers to "gimme a few days" he returned to his office in Portland.

In Toronto, Chief Grasett received a collect telegram from

Fortune and was reluctant to accept it, the police budget being overspent because of the Small case. But since it was from a police department he finally gave in and accepted the wire. Informed about the man Cooper, he wrote Fortune to continue the investigation and try to pinpoint the identity. The letter arrived by train and postal carrier on October 15, 1920. In the letter, Grasett requested Fortune to pick Cooper up and question him and also make a search of the man's lodgings in an attempt to find the missing bonds. A check on deposit vaults and savings accounts at local banks might also reveal evidence of the bonds or of a large amount of money in the name of Cooper, or of Doughty.

Fortune wired Grasett, again collect, about the fifth of November, stating that he had no jurisdiction in the case. The man Cooper had a responsible auditing and treasurer's position with a powerful lumber company and there was no legal right to question him or raid his premises. However, a recent letter to Cooper from Toronto mentioned a woman called Jeannie, and the post office at the camp said that Cooper had received a number of letters from Canada. Would that be of interest?

"Jeannie," exclaimed Grasett. "Why, that's Jeannie Doughty!"

Calling Austin Mitchell, he said: "Get a ticket for Portland, Oregon. Doughty may be there."

Mitchell hadn't a clue where Portland was located, and while Grand Trunk Railway agents were booking his route through Chicago to Denver and Portland, Chief Grasett managed to squeeze enough money for Mitchell's return trip and one single, in case they were on the right track.

The trip took Mitchell eight days. He arrived in Portland on the morning of November 19, and by that afternoon was studying Charlie Cooper. He watched him at work through a crack in an office door. He followed him at a distance when Cooper went to the staff cookhouse for dinner. He watched him eat, kept an eye on him while he read the evening newspaper in the staff lounge, and tried to identify his characteristics with those of Doughty in so far as the latter were known to police. Only the height of Cooper seemed to fit the description exactly. He had no mustache. His hair was thinned almost to baldness, unlike the shock of dark hair in the photograph on the poster. But the weight was reasonably close, though Cooper appeared to be slightly heavier. There was only one solution, and Mitchell knew it. He would have to accost Cooper and get some answers.

With Fortune beside him, Mitchell followed Cooper out of the building, catching up to him as he walked slowly over the sawdust pathway to the staff bunkhouse. Cooper never turned around, never saw the two men following him. He did not appear nervous or apprehensive. Mitchell was having second thoughts about his quarry.

Just as Cooper was turning toward the wooden steps that led upward and into the bunkhouse, Mitchell was right behind him, so close he could hear his breathing. The soft sawdust, damp from almost continual rain, muffled the footsteps.

Mitchell reached forward and tapped Cooper on the shoulder and at the same time greeted him with: "Hello Jack! How are you?"

Cooper stopped, his left foot already on the first step. He pulled his foot back and slowly, ever so slowly, turned to face the man who had just spoken to him. The two men looked at one another.

"I'm Detective Sergeant Mitchell from Toronto."

The man called Cooper swayed as if overcome by dizziness. His knees sagged and he slipped to the wet sawdust, and without looking at Mitchell he blurted out: "I'm Doughty. . . . I'm the man you're looking for."

When he recovered from the shock, Doughty, accompanied by Mitchell, went to the bedroom and packed a small bag.

"How did you find me?" he asked with an unbelieving look on his face.

"From a Toronto letter to you," laughed Mitchell. "Someone here in the camp saw the postmark and then saw your photo in Portland. So, Jack, the running is over. You must feel relieved."

"Not a bit," snapped Doughty. That was the last time he spoke until his arrival in Toronto on November 28 to be greeted by a horde of newsmen and press photographers and a large crowd of people.

While flash powder exploded in the Union Station lobby, voices raised in anger and shouts of curiosity greeted Doughty with "Where's Ambrose? . . . What have you done to Small? . . . Where is Small buried? . . . Is it Theresa you love?"

"Let's get him out of here," Mitchell told police constables. "Some of these people are in an angry mood. I didn't expect this."

Mitchell told the press there would be no interviews. Doughty would be permitted to see his sisters and his two sons and then he was to be booked and kept in Don Jail. At headquarters, Doughty was charged with the theft of the bonds.

The only words he said were: "I want a lawyer."

At the Don Jail, Inspector Hammond questioned him briefly. "Where is Ambrose Small?"

"I have not the slightest idea."

"You knew that he was missing?"

"Yes, when I returned to Toronto from Montreal, but Mrs. Small said he had run away with a woman."

"What did you talk to Mrs. Small about on those occasions?"

"That's none of your business."

"We'll see whether it's my business or not, and you may be charged with Mr. Small's disappearance."

Doughty did not reply, but when asked if he knew about the missing bonds, he at once said that he did.

"They are in a bag at my sister's house on Kingsmount Road."

"Why did you steal them?"

"I didn't steal them, they were given to me by Mr. Small as a reward for my many years of service."

"Then why did you run to Oregon, if everything was so up and up?"

"That's my business. Get me a lawyer."

Accompanied by Hammond, Guthrie and Mitchell, Doughty was driven to Kingsmount Road where he was permitted to greet his sisters and his sons. He asked Jeannie to get him the package which he had entrusted to her when he left Toronto on December 2. She returned with a brown paper bag, not unlike an ordinary grocery bag. Mitchell opened it and out tumbled a number of green-coloured certificates.

Counting them later in police headquarters, Mitchell said the bonds were intact and totalled $100,000. Accrued interest on the attached coupons made the package worth approximately $104,000.

Back again in the Don Jail, Doughty refused to answer any of Mitchell's further questions and again called for a lawyer.

Toronto and Ontario police thought that Doughty should be charged with a more serious crime than just bond-stealing. With Small not around to testify, there were some in the Attorney General's department who did not believe there was sufficient evidence for a conviction on the bond theft, since according to Doughty nothing had been stolen, and who but Theresa was to refute this? Theresa's evidence that Doughty had no right to the bonds might or might not stand up in court since there was no corroborating evidence that the bonds had been stolen. Nor was there any evidence that Small had given them to Doughty—no signed documents, no promise before witnesses. And as everyone knew, Small was not a man to give money away.

Since there was no body, Doughty could not be charged with murder. But the police believed that Doughty's alleged attempts to get others to help him kidnap or kill Small were sufficient evidence of conspiracy, and that this, tied to the evidence of the fight in the furnace room and the taking of the bonds, would be enough for a conviction that would salt Doughty away for life.

He was therefore charged with conspiracy to kidnap Small. He appeared for a preliminary hearing on both charges before Magistrate Denison at the City Hall in Toronto and was remanded for trial by judge and jury. The conspiracy charge was withdrawn when the Attorney General of Ontario was assured by his staff that there was no evidence of conspiracy on the December 2 date. Doughty would face the theft charge only.

The announcement that he would face trial and cross-examination on the Small case lured scores of newsmen from all parts of the United States and Canada and several from Great Britain. It was expected to be a spectacular trial, particularly since Theresa Small herself would appear to testify.

Owing to a number of remands by both defence and prosecution, the trial was postponed until March 21, 1921. The Toronto City Hall area became a scene that was reminiscent of Hanging Day in a western cowtown.

Time of the trial was set for ten o'clock, but three hours before that, spectators began to gather on the lawns and in the corridors hoping to catch a glimpse of the principals in the greatest local mystery of the century. Hundreds who lined up for admission to the courtroom were to be disappointed. News reporters were given preferential seating as were members of the Doughty, Small and Kormann families and a large number of law students from nearby Osgoode Hall.

Judge William Denton presided. Unlike many judges, Denton permitted the press to rearrange the seating so as to get as close as possible to the witness stand without interfering with the large oaken table set aside for the defence and prosecution attorneys. Photographers were not permitted to enter but Judge Denton posed for his photograph with the lawyers just before the doors of the courtroom were thrown open to the selected visitors at 9:55 a.m.

There was a sound of shouting outside the building and seconds later the sound continued into the corridors. John Doughty had arrived for his trial. It was ten o'clock sharp.

Doughty was accompanied by Jeannie, who clung tightly to his arm. As they walked through the long corridors between the lines of spectators, there were a few calls of derision and sporadic clapping as well.

Theresa had not arrived when the courtroom doors were closed by the sheriff on duty. Howls of anguish reverberated through the halls as the crowd realized that the trial was closed to the public, and shouts of "secret trial" and "no justice for Doughty" echoed through the building. There was pushing and shoving, and extra police were called to keep order. So great was the noise from the irate crowd that order could not be maintained in the courtroom and Judge Denton was obliged to call a fifteen-minute recess until police could clear the hallways.

At 10:30, order was restored and the judge re-entered the courtroom. The clerk of the court brought the trial to order by his familiar shout of "Silence", followed by "Oyez . . . oyez . . . oyez. . . . Draw near and ye shall be heard."

Judge Denton waited until the courtroom was silent. He nodded to the clerk to begin.

"John Doughty . . . answer to your name."

"Here, your honour."

"You, John Doughty, of the City of Toronto and of the County of York, stand indicted for the crime of theft, to wit, the theft of bonds totalling approximately one hundred and four thousand dollars, the property of Ambrose and Theresa Small; on or about the Second of December in the Year of Our Lord, Nineteen Hundred and Nineteen. How do you plead?"

"Not guilty."

Between thirty and forty newsmen rushed for the hallway to get the flash over the telephone lines to their newsrooms. The City Hall press room was on the second floor of the old building, on the same level as the courtrooms, and the pounding of feet could be heard a block away.

Judge Denton was not disturbed by these flurries. He had an excellent rapport with newsmen and he also knew of the international interest in the Doughty trial. He patiently waited until quietness was once more restored before starting the procedure of selecting twelve men for the petit jury.

Doughty was permitted to sit at the "defence table" with his attorneys, I.F. Hellmuth, K.C., and Miss Clara Brett Martin. At an adjoining table sat Frank Hughes, attorney for the Small estate, and beyond him crown counsel, Colonel R.H. Greer in charge of the prosecution and Toronto Crown Attorney Eric Armour, assisting.

Doughty's bail bond of $5,000 was returned to Hellmuth, and Judge Denton called in the volunteers for the petit jury.

The empanelling of the jury had hardly begun when a great commotion occurred beyond the courtroom and in the hallways leading to the entrance of the court. At first, it sounded like a mob gathering on Bastille Day. But suddenly it became a deafening challenge of shouts and screams and the sounds of fighting. Judge Denton again called a recess and at that moment the mob burst into the courtroom.

Even with the assistance of City Hall constables, it was difficult for courtroom sheriffs and bailiffs to break up the mob. It was finally determined that the creator of the uproar was a woman. She had stirred up the crowd outside the courtroom by saying that Ambrose Small was still alive; that she had seen him a year ago, had talked to him, and that he was a prisoner of kidnappers and could be freed for a million dollars but Theresa wouldn't pay it.

At the very moment this unnamed woman was haranguing the crowd, already sullen and angered by the closing of the courtroom doors, Theresa Small walked in with her sister Josephine. The shouting woman turned and pointed a finger at Theresa.

"That's her," she screeched. "She wouldn't pay a million for her husband."

The mob surged forward with a low rumble, harbinger of a riot.

"They'll hang poor Doughty for this," screamed the woman, and she marched toward the courtroom door with the crowd around her chanting: "Freedom for Jack!"

Others outside the City Hall, and those gathered in curious groups near the clock tower, heard the roaring crowd and in seconds were rushing into the building to join the fray. Most of those caught in the melee were uncertain of what was going on, but shouts that Small was alive seemed to spur them onward into the trial courtroom. Before the scene was finally cleared away, the mysterious woman who started it all had disappeared.

"Another crazy woman," said the police, and shrugged.

It took until noontime to select the jury, the prosecution challenging ten of the jurors and the defence challenging twelve. One juror, who swore he had some knowledge of the case, was dismissed from duty. During this phase of the trial proceedings, Theresa and Josephine attempted to gain entrance to the courtroom but were denied admittance by the City Hall sheriffs and it took the intervention of the Crown Attorney to get them a seat. Later, the judge explained to the press that the confusion was caused by "over-zealous bailiffs."

Before the lunch break, Mr. Greer presented the "case for the Crown," which was a general outline of the association between Doughty and Small, the events of December 2, 1919, when Doughty left Toronto for Montreal and the new job, the subsequent search for Doughty, and the discovery of the missing bonds. He asked the jury to confine themselves to the evidence regarding the bonds and nothing else in reaching a verdict, which he suggested had to be "guilty."

Towering over the jury with his tremendous frame, a shock of unruly hair moving like waves when he moved and a voice that shook the courtroom with fist-pounding adjectives, Mr. Greer declared the evidence would be clear, that John Doughty removed bonds that belonged to Ambrose and Theresa Small without their knowledge or permission and then deliberately hid them until such time as he could cash them without fear of being apprehended.

The first witness at the trial, stockbroker J.H.F. Timmins, had known Small for fifteen years. He testified that he had sold Ambrose a hundred thousand dollars' worth of bonds in 1918 and they were to mature in 1933. He said the bonds were ordered in ten-thousand-dollar amounts and the money transfer was made through the Dominion Bank at Small's request.

Questioned by Mr. Hellmuth, the broker could not explain why the final delivery of the bonds was in thousand-dollar lots instead of the ten-thousand lots ordered by Small.

"Could it be Small changed his mind for easy cashing purposes?"

"I have no idea. I placed the order with the Dominion Bank and why the change took place I cannot say," concluded the broker.

Thomas Joyce, assistant manager of the bank, produced a document showing the denomination change but there was no signature for the change. He also produced a copy of the Small Ledger and it revealed a deposit of $137.50 made on the day before Small's disappearance. But the deposit slip for this amount could not be traced. Under cross-examination, the bank official presumed that the amount "could be the interest for six months on a $5,000 bond" but he had no knowledge of this bond and the interest did not come from the coupons of the stolen group as none had been clipped.

The next witness brought an unusual silence over the proceedings. Each of the twelve jurymen sat upright and listened intently as Fred Miller, keeper of the safety-deposit boxes at the Dominion Bank, revealed the comings and goings of Doughty to the vaults in December 1919. There was also another secret to be revealed.

"Mr. Small's box number was 1564," he testified, producing a signed document from Small permitting John Doughty access to that box number. The witness also revealed that Doughty had a safety-deposit vault of his own, Number 2550.

"Did John Doughty visit the vault on December 2 or thereabouts?" asked Mr. Greer.

"Yes, sir. Mr. Doughty went to Mr. Small's box at 2:36 p.m. on the afternoon of December 1, 1919, and signed out at 2:48 p.m. On that same day, but later, at 3:32 to be precise, he had access to Mr. Small's box and departed at 3:40 p.m. Then, the next day, that would be December 2, he entered the vault at 9:59 a.m. and left at 10:02 a.m."

"Did you have any occasion to speak with the accused?"

"Yes, Mr. Doughty asked what steps he should take to appoint a deputy to open the personal box and I believe I handed him a card to be filled out."

"When did the accused return to the vault after those dates?"

"There is no further signature on the admission document until May 6, 1920, and that was for Mr. Doughty's personal box."

"You mean John Doughty was in the bank on that date?"

The jury leaned forward. Pencils on press notepads ceased to move.

"No, sir, but Miss Jean Doughty came to the vault and presented a letter signed by John Doughty on December 2, 1919, giving her permission to open his box. The note said that she would share in box 2550 from that date onward."

"What did Miss Doughty say to you?" pressed Greer.

Defence counsel Hellmuth jumped to his feet.

"I object, your honour . . . we don't want any third-person evidence here. Besides, Miss Doughty is not on trial."

He was overruled and Greer asked the question again, only to learn that Miller was not on duty in the vault at the noon hour when Miss Doughty showed up. She worked at the Dominion Munitions Board, down the street from the bank.

"Who was on duty?"

The witness explained that a clerk by the name of Slattery was on duty and that this clerk refused to permit Jeannie to "sign in" and kept the letter and two signed cards for an official answer.

When he returned from lunch, Miller said, he was handed the documents and when Miss Doughty returned to the bank a short time later, he told her he could not give her permission to enter the vault.

"Why not?" asked the defence counsel Hellmuth.

"Well, Mr. Small's disappearance and all . . . and Mr. Doughty's disappearance. . . . I thought the opening of the box should come from a higher source than myself."

"Did Miss Doughty say why she had the letter and the cards and for what purpose they were entrusted to her by her brother?"

"She said he wanted her to share the vault because he would be in Montreal."

"What then?"

"I sent Miss Doughty to the assistant manager and he denied her access."

Mr. Greer asked permission to pose another question to Miller and was told to go ahead.

"How big was the Doughty safety-deposit box? Was it big enough to hold the missing bonds for which the accused is charged?"

"No, Mr. Greer, the Doughty box was the smallest one we rent, not near big enough to hold the bonds."

Following a fifteen-minute recess, Jeannie Doughty took the witness stand.

Newsmen described Jeannie Doughty as a "plain woman," a "comely woman," a "matron" who was "once pretty" but had now "slipped into middle age ungraciously."

She was forty-seven, three years older than her brother John. Her eyes were pale blue and her light auburn hair was brushed rearward under a tight-fitting dark felt hat. She appeared to be shy and her damp hands showed a slight trace of nervousness. It was evident from the beginning of her cross-examination that the Crown considered Jeannie a prime witness in the case.

The prosecution thrust a letter into her hands.

"Is that your handwriting?"

"Yes, Mr. Greer."

"Who did you write that letter to?"

"My brother."

"When?"

"On December 21."

"Where was John at that time?"

"In Montreal."

"Then tell me, what did you mean when you wrote, and I

am quoting your words from this letter, 'your flying visit has relieved my mind of a great burden'?"

"I meant that I was relieved to know that we wouldn't have to move the boys to Montreal, his sons that is, and they would remain with me and my sister."

"Was that the great burden?"

"Yes."

"I suggest to you, Miss Doughty, that the great burden was the bonds that your brother handed you for safe keeping."

Mr. Hellmuth objected to this assertion by the Crown and demanded to have the letter returned to Jeannie and the contents stricken from the court record.

"That letter must have been stolen from her and I demand to know how Mr. Greer got it," he said, his face flushed with anger.

"None of your business!" shouted Mr. Greer, and the two lawyers engaged in a heated controversy over the letter as it had not been seized by court order or gained by a police search warrant.

Judge Denton was asked to rule on the letter's admissibility; he declared in favour of the Crown and asked the prosecution to continue.

"You had the bonds in your possession."

"They were in the house."

"Were you not worried about those bonds?"

"Yes, from the time that Jack gave them to me on December 2, I was worried about them."

"Did you know who was the real owner of the bonds?"

"Mr. Small."

"Did your brother say they had been given to him?"

"Yes, for his long years of service."

"Did you believe him?"

Mr. Hellmuth objected and the judge agreed and asked Greer to change his line of questioning.

"In any event, you knew of the bonds and you put them away for your brother at his request, correct?"

"Yes."

"During his December visits did you talk about the bonds?"

"Yes, I asked him to return them to Mr. Small."

"And what was his answer?" pressed the Crown.

"Jack said he couldn't return them to Mr. Small."

"Did he tell you why he couldn't?"

"No."

"I suggest to you, witness, he told you he couldn't because Small was dead."

The uproar that followed this charge by Mr. Greer made it impossible to continue the trial for forty-five minutes. The jury was dismissed and legal arguments broke out between the four attorneys and the judge. When the jury returned, the uproar started again but Judge Denton thought that Mr. Greer had a right to pursue his line of questioning if he was attempting to prove a conspiracy between the brother and sister in hiding stolen property.

"He couldn't return them . . . was it because he knew Small was dead?" persisted Mr. Greer, over the continued protests of lawyer Hellmuth. ". . . and therefore you knew it also . . . you knew Small was dead?"

The noise of newsmen running for telephones and their wire services thundered through the corridors, but the rapid-fire questioning was continued by Greer, who was considered the top criminal lawyer in Canada.

"No, no, I didn't know what he meant," sobbed the witness.

"Oh yes you did, but you were out to protect your brother, no matter what the circumstances. . . . Now isn't that right?"

"This is brutal, plain brutal," shouted Hellmuth, jumping to his feet.

"Continue, Mr. Greer," said the judge.

"Didn't John tell you that he was the only man in the world who knew that Small could not get the bonds back . . . didn't he?"

"Yes," sobbed the witness.

"Then, if you have no explanation, or do not wish to provide an explanation, let me tell you that John Doughty was the only man who really knew where Small was."

"These innuendoes have no place here," shouted Hellmuth, pounding the defence table. "Doughty is charged with theft . . . he has admitted to having the bonds. . . . Stop this cruelty to this lady."

Judge Denton agreed. He ordered the Crown to stop engaging in arguments with the witness and confine the questions to the bonds. Turning to the sobbing witness, he asked her to tell her story of the bonds as she knew it and there would be no further cross-examination concerning Small.

When she had calmed herself, Jeannie told the jury that she had suffered a "terrible strain" during the absence of her brother, knowing about the bonds and suspecting they didn't belong to him. She said she made repeated attempts to have them returned to Mrs. Small but her phone calls went unanswered. Finally she sent her sister, Mrs. Lovatt, to Mrs. Small's home on Glen Road with the box of bonds, but Mrs. Small refused to see Mrs. Lovatt.

The witness began to cry again and it was obvious to the judge that she would be unable to continue that afternoon.

"Miss Doughty can be recalled tomorrow . . . she has been a fine witness as far as this court is concerned but I think she needs a rest. . . . Who is the next witness, Mr. Greer?"

"Ernest Reid, your honour. He was operating chocolate-vending machines at the Grand Opera House for about twelve years. He also operated vending machines in other Small theatres and he may recall some discussions he had with

Doughty over bonds, which I think may be pertinent to this case."

"Take the witness stand, Mr. Reid," ordered the judge. "Just tell us simply what you know about bonds being mentioned in conversations with the accused."

Reid swore that in the fall of 1919, about six or seven weeks before Small's disappearance, Doughty invited him into the theatre office to discuss a "business proposition." Doughty suggested to Reid that the latter could get "something" out of a business deal that Small was at the moment negotiating if Reid would join Doughty in a scheme.

Reid said he listened without comment. He didn't like Doughty and didn't trust him, either. Doughty said that both of them could get a fair share of these negotiations from some bonds from which Small was clipping all the coupons.

"I remember Doughty saying: 'We both work for Small and you get nothing and I get nothing.' "

Under cross-examination by Hellmuth, Reid said the negotiations referred to by Doughty had something to do with Small buying or selling a lease of some sort but he was never quite sure. Doughty told him that the chance to be rewarded for their years of work was rapidly slipping away and they would have to work fast to get their "just deserts."

"Doughty never did explain to me the circumstances," he said.

"You're not sure of your dates, either," snapped Hellmuth. "The property that Doughty was talking to you about was in the spring of 1919 and it was purchased by Small at that time. . . . Surely that doesn't surprise you—or does it?"

"I gave the dates as honestly as I remember."

"Would you agree there could be as much as six months' difference in the time you had this conversation with Doughty over property and bonds?"

The witness became bewildered under the pressure of the rapid-fire questioning by the defence counsel but he answered: "I couldn't swear when it was. . . . It isn't even clear to me now when the conversation took place."

"It seemed clear enough when Mitchell helped you put together the statement," Hellmuth replied with thin sarcasm.

"I certainly object to that snide remark," snapped the prosecutor. "This witness gave his statement to Mitchell without threat or promise."

"Ho, ho, ho," retorted the defence.

"Now, now, Mr. Hellmuth," the judge remarked.

"Why, you honour, this witness doesn't know when he talked to Doughty, not the month and perhaps not even the year. Of what importance is this man, nothing. I say, absolutely nothing."

"He heard mention, in any event, the fact that bonds were available for something or other . . . certainly to make money that was owing from past work or from being underpaid, or something," observed the judge.

"Yes, your honour, but the way the answers to simple questions are coming, it is obvious the witness has been prompted what to say."

"Nonsense," growled Greer, loud enough for the crowd outside the courtroom to hear.

"Well then, let's see how much he might have been assisted or influenced," retorted Hellmuth. He reached for the questions and answers supplied by the Crown, which were taken under oath in police headquarters in February, 1921, between Mitchell and Reid.

"Mr. Reid, do you remember being questioned by Detective Mitchell four weeks ago?"

"Yes."

"You swore at that time that Doughty made a proposition to

you in the fall of 1919 to get hold of some bonds . . . but now you agree your timetable may have been out as much as six months, is that not correct?"

"Yes, some of the things you say that I said don't sound like I said them," replied Reid and the members of the jury giggled.

"Did you say these words: 'Doughty knew what was going on and I asked John what was he being given for all the things he had done for Small' . . . Did you say those words and are they your language?"

"No, I don't recall saying that."

"You didn't make that statement to Mitchell?"

"No."

"Or anyone else?"

"No."

"Did you say that if Small didn't give anything to Doughty as a reward for his negotiations, that you wouldn't do anything for Small again . . . did you make that statement to Mitchell?"

"Yes sir, I made that statement."

"Did you enter into any agreement on that occasion with Doughty or enter any scheme to get something from Mr. Small?"

"No, sir."

"Did Detective Mitchell write the questions and ask you if they were true or false?"

"He asked me a lot of questions."

"But he was mostly concerned with the mention of the bonds, was he not?"

"Oh, come now," sneered Greer. "This was a regular interrogation of the witness, to try and find a clue to the disappearance of Mr. Small and the attitude of Doughty toward Small . . . and if the matter of bonds came up it was natural for Mitchell to press for further information. I would consider this correct police investigative procedure, Mr. Hellmuth."

"If Reid's dates are six months out, his evidence is absolutely worthless and I'm now beginning to wonder whether there ever was any conversation between Doughty and Reid," retorted the defence counsel.

"The jury can determine the credibility of the witnesses, Mr. Hellmuth," replied the judge, who then recessed the case to the following morning at ten o'clock.

Chapter Nine

Jeannie Doughty was recalled to the witness stand on the second day of the trial. She appeared composed and smiled at the jury.

"Miss Doughty," began prosecutor Greer, "I want to talk to you about your brother's actions on that December 2, 1919, just prior to his going to Montreal, if, in fact, he went to Montreal . . . did you take him to the Union Station that night?"

"Yes, but I drove Jack to the Grand Opera House first because he said he had to pick up some letters that were in his office."

"Did he finally come out of the theatre?"

"Of course."

"What letters did you see in his possession?"

"None."

"What letters did you see him post?"

"I didn't see him post any."

"What do you think, then, he was doing in the theatre, now that you have had time to think over the details of that night?"

"I have no idea, I'm not one of Mr. Mitchell's mind-reading friends."

"What happened next?"

"I drove Jack to the Union Station."

"Go on."

"He handed me a brown paper bag and he said that it belonged to Mr. Small and he told me that if I didn't hear from him in the next few days, I was to put the parcel in a safety-deposit box and he told me not to open the parcel as it was the private property of Mr. Small."

"Did you walk into the station with him?"

"No, I dropped him at the front entrance."

"Was there any other conversation?"

"No."

"What mood was your brother in . . . happy . . . sad . . . depressed?"

"He didn't want to go to Montreal and leave his boys and me and the family . . . we have always been closely knit."

"He was morose?"

"He was sad and a little bewildered by all the sudden events, I think."

"So you bade him farewell?"

"Yes."

"And you drove home with the brown paper package on the seat beside you?"

"Yes, Mr. Greer."

"What did you do with it that night?"

"I put it in the chiffonier."

Later she went to the Bank of Montreal, she testified, and obtained a safety-deposit box for which she paid three dollars rent, but the box was too small to hold the package.

"What would it have cost to get a box that would be big enough to hold the parcel?"

Miss Doughty replied that she made no further inquiries. She decided not to put the parcel in a deposit box at all for two or three days.

"Why?"

"Well, Jack told me at the station that it would only be for two or three days."

"And this is the first time you have remembered that remark?"

"Well I always understood—"

"Never mind what you understood—tell us what he said."

She stuck to her statement that "it would be only a few days."

It was on December 21 that she next saw her brother, and though he had been home at 8 Kingsmount Road nearly all day she did not speak to him about the parcel.

"Did you know they were bonds?"

"No, not at that time."

Other persons were in the house, so that opportunities for conversation about the parcel were limited, and when she finally went upstairs to talk to him he was asleep. He had gone out earlier in the afternoon to be vaccinated because of the quarantine regulations in Montreal.

Later when he awoke the conversation centred around Small's disappearance.

Finally Mr. Greer drew from the witness a reference to the parcel as "valuable papers."

Stepping briskly up to the witness box, the crown prosecutor dramatically pointed his finger at the prisoner's sister. "He told you they were valuable papers?"

"Not on that occasion."

"How did he designate them?"

"He did not designate or describe them. He did not say what made them valuable."

"Was there anything that occurred between you and John on December 21 that tended to relieve your mind?"

"No—I was not worrying."

"Not worrying?"

"Well, not much."

"But you worried a little?" pursued the prosecutor. "Why did you not discuss it before the family?"

"Because he had told me not to mention it to anyone."

"What conversation passed between Mrs. Small and your brother on December 21? Did you hear any of it over the telephone?"

"No."

"Did you suggest that he should telephone to Mrs. Small?"

"No, why should I?"

"Never mind why should you. . . . With the awful burden on your mind what did you do with the package?"

"What do you mean?" demanded Miss Doughty.

"What would *you* mean by that question?" retorted Mr. Greer. "What did you do with the package?"

"It was in the chiffonier."

"How long did it remain in the chiffonier?"

"Until December 29."

The witness said that her brother had returned from Montreal on Saturday, December 27.

"What did you say to him that Saturday?"

"Very little."

"What time did he arrive?"

"I will not say."

"Just what do you mean by 'I will not say'?"

"She means she cannot say the exact time," interrupted the judge.

"No conversation took place over that parcel on December 27?"

"Nothing."

"But you knew there were bonds inside that package, right?"

"Yes, I had opened it and I told my brother Will about it."

"All right, what about December 28—that would be Sunday, the day he was to return to Montreal?"

"I asked him about the bonds and when I told him they

were made out to Mr. Small and why didn't he return them, Jack said he couldn't."

"Oh, he did, did he? . . . said he could not return them to Small."

"Yes, he said he had not had the opportunity to see Mr. Small and could not return them."

"You have made two statements, Miss Doughty . . . first that he told you he could not return the bonds and, second, that he had no opportunity to return them . . . which one is correct?"

"It amounts to the same thing," she quipped. "Jack said he no longer had the key to the safety boxes and couldn't return them."

"Yes, that's another explanation," sneered Greer. "What happened to the bonds that day after you and your brother talked them over?"

"I took them to the attic to hide them and I placed them under the floorboards."

"How did you get them under a floor?" snapped Greer.

"The floor in the attic was unfinished and I placed them under the . . . what do you call them . . . the rafters."

"You mean the joists," said Mr. Hellmuth.

"Did you know the value of those bonds at this time?" asked Greer.

"Yes, altogether, they totalled about $105,000."

"Now tell us, Miss Doughty, you had conversations with your brother about bonds that belonged to Mr. Small and the huge amount they were worth. What explanation did he give you for having these bonds in his possession?"

"He said he took the bonds out of the bank while cutting coupons as he thought it an opportune time to speak to Mr. Small about his promise. But Mr. Small had disappeared and he could not do so."

"And of course he could not turn the bonds over to the police?" countered Mr. Greer.

The next change affecting the bonds came on May 24th, 1920. On that day Jeannie consulted her brother Will about the hiding place in the rafters, she admitted.

"What made you want to change their hiding place?"

"Well, Detective Sergeant Mitchell had been to the house looking around, and I got excited."

"And you lost your head?"

Mr. Hellmuth protested and asked that protection be given the witness in connection with any evidence she might give as to her own involvement.

"Quite agreeable," smiled Mr. Greer. "She can have a universal order of protection so far as I am concerned."

Mr. Hellmuth also protested against evidence being taken on what Miss Doughty had done with the bonds. "She is not on trial. I submit that such evidence has nothing to do with this case. It simply serves to prejudice the case."

Judge Denton: "I do not think that anything is being prejudiced. The evidence is admissible. Proceed."

Miss Doughty then described how she had handed the bonds over to Will Doughty on the morning of May 24th.

"I told Will I did not want anything more to do with the bonds," she testified. And after handing them over to him she ran from the house. She had not seen them again or known where they were until November 29th, the day after John Doughty was returned to Toronto.

"Did you ever talk about the bonds in your house?"

"Yes, thousands of times."

"A constant topic of conversation?"

"The responsibility of those bonds was something terrible."

"And that responsibility was on your shoulders?"

"It was on *our* shoulders," she answered.

"And where was the man that gave you the bonds to keep for him?"

Deliberately and slowly she replied, "That I did not know at any time."

"Did he communicate with any person you know of in Toronto?"

"He did with my brother Will."

"What was that date?"

"I don't know."

"Was it after he left Toronto?"

"It was after December 29th."

"How long after?"

"I don't know."

"At his home?"

"Yes."

She never saw the letters, she swore.

"Were you told at any time where your brother John was?"

"No."

"Are you sure?"

"Yes."

She had no connection with him nor did she know where he had gone until he returned with Detective Mitchell, she testified.

"Did you say anything to Mitchell at any time about the bonds?"

"Mr. Mitchell inferred that Small's bonds were in Jack's box."

"Did you tell him where the bonds were?"

"I didn't know then. How could I?"

"Why didn't you take them to the police in the first place?"

She replied that she did not tell the police because "we thought Mrs. Small was the proper authority to take them, but she would not receive Mrs. Lovatt."

"Can you tell me anything else we could have done with

them?" asked the witness, after the Crown suggested that because Mrs. Small would not accept the bonds they were kept hidden.

"Did you write a letter to the police department officials at any time concerning the bonds?"

"Certainly not."

"Did you communicate with the Attorney General?"

"We thought that Christmastime would be a good time to pass them on to authorities. We thought that would be the only available chance of getting them out of our hands without detectives or anyone knowing anything about them." (She meant the bonds would be in a box that would be wrapped for Christmas.)

"So John's arrest before Christmas forestalled that intention?"

"Yes."

Witness then revealed that the bonds were turned over to Mitchell at the Lovatt house when all the Doughty family were present.

Chapter Ten

The afternoon of the second day wound up the trial. A long parade of friends and associates of Small and Doughty told how the two fought bitterly over the years, particularly over money matters which included Theresa's lavish spending and Doughty's wages.

When Theresa Small took the witness stand and was sworn in by the clerk of the court, a hush settled over the busy courtroom. Reporters held their pencils in anticipation. Lawyers and their assistants, the jury and a large number of law students and past witnesses watched and listened. But they were to be disappointed. Theresa was only on the witness stand for a matter of seconds.

She told Mr. Greer that Doughty was not an associate of her husband but a mere employee. However, he had been entrusted with a key to the safety-deposit box because a number of theatre booking contracts were kept there. And besides, Small trusted Doughty.

"Would Mr. Small have given Doughty those bonds?" asked the crown prosecutor.

"Amby wouldn't have given away ten cents unless he was getting twenty cents back," she said coldly.

Theresa never looked toward the prisoner's box while she was in the witness stand. She smiled to the jury and to Mr.

Greer as she stepped down from the witness stand and departed.

"That puts the position of John Doughty in the correct slot," prosecutor Greer declared in his address to the jury.

"There has never been any dispute as to who was the owner of the bonds. John Doughty was not a partner. He was not an associate but an employee and the first principle of employment is that the employee should be faithful to his employer.

"The document that Small gave Doughty on January 15, 1918, filed here as an exhibit, was a permission only to deal with those bonds as a servant of his master, and in his employer's interest, not in the interest of John Doughty but in the interests of A. J. Small," he declared.

Mr. Greer stated that he would "run over" the evidence of all the witnesses but would concentrate his remarks on the testimony of Jeannie Doughty.

He noted with sarcasm that John Doughty did not take the witness stand to defend himself against the charge. Mr. Greer pointed out that, under the Common Law, Doughty was not required to take the witness stand but if he had, he would have been subject to cross-examination.

"You may be curious about the Power of Attorney that Small's document gave to Doughty," said the prosecutor, speaking in low tones with sympathetic resonance in his voice.

"That power of attorney did not give Doughty any power to deal in an unauthorized manner with his employer's bonds, to hold them improperly, or for a longer period than was in his employer's interest. Mrs. Small had told police officers that Doughty was not another member of the family in relationship to the vault but a servant with an employment contract to perform certain duties.

"I thought it significant, and you may or may not agree with me, but you will recall in the evidence from the bank records that on December 1, 1919, when Small was alive, it took

Doughty eight minutes to get the bonds from the vault; but on December 2, the day Small disappeared, Doughty was in an awful hurry and it only took him three minutes to get his work done in the vault. Yes, he was a man in a hurry and the record shows it.

"Let me deal for a moment with the testimony of Ernest Reid. It is apparent that all that was wicked in Doughty's mind was revealed in Reid's evidence. Yes, Doughty had it in his mind for a year or more, this wicked plan. Doughty said to Reid: 'You're not going to get a thing out of this,' paving the way for his proposition. Then he told Reid about the bonds and Reid says he suggested that two smart men might frame up a plan to get some of those bonds. Then Doughty told him to go home and think it over for a few days.

"Is that the conduct of a faithful employee? If you found an employee of yours standing outside your door, stopping strangers and suggesting to them that they should join him in trying to get possession of his employer's property, what would you think of your employee?" he asked.

Turning toward the defence table and pointing his finger at Doughty, Greer shouted: "This man, doing all these things, disclosed the treachery and blackness of his heart."

The prosecutor reminded the jury that Doughty told his sister that he had remained in the Grand office until after six that December 2; he told Theresa Small that he left at 5:30. Jeannie said he ran into the office later that night to get "important papers," and lawyer Flock said he left Small at 5:30 and saw no sign of Doughty at any time.

"How can you believe this man . . . but, then, it's up to you to sift the evidence and discover what you believe to be the truth based on reasonable assumption," he thundered.

Turning to Jeannie Doughty's evidence, Mr. Greer asked: "Do you believe that her brother came to Toronto from

Montreal on December 21 simply to get vaccinated . . . or do you believe that he came to discuss a very important matter, as her letter to him on December 23 would indicate?

Why "a flying trip" and what was the "awful burden" mentioned in the letter, asked Mr. Greer, who alluded to Miss Doughty's hesitancy on the stand and her reply that the "awful burden" lifted from her mind was that they would not have to go to Montreal to live. The Crown inferred that a much more important matter lay concealed behind the suggested purpose of the trip.

Mr. Greer referred to Jean Doughty as having "a laudable sense of loyalty, but a disastrous sense of morality."

"When on May 24 Miss Doughty handed the bonds to her brother Will after telling Mrs. Lovatt what they were and telling them not to tell her what they would do with them, was that the honest act of a sister who knows she is doing something for an honest brother?

"You have got to say this about Doughty—he took the most cowardly course he could have taken in regard to those bonds. He went away to Montreal and left them in the hands of this girl, whom we must admire for her loyalty to him. If he had been honest and clean in the sight of his God, why did he not take them to Montreal with him?

"Then he went thirty-two hundred miles away, he changed his name, he was away eleven months, and he was not caught until thirteen thousand circulars had been sent out.

"He left a job at seventy-five dollars a week, and he left the line of work for which he had for fifteen years been fitting himself, and he went down to a lumber camp to take a hard job at menial labour. Is that the conduct of anybody but a guilty man?

"If you men of the jury had a hired man and sent him to the bank for two hundred dollars, and that man disappeared with your money, was caught later, and, being brought back, explained that he had just put the money away, would you believe him?

"Is it conceivable that a man who knew himself honest would go away and hide himself like that, except to hide from a crime? The conscience that God has given us to act like a compass in the darkness of the night—this conscience that makes cowards of us all, made a coward of John Doughty, and sent him out as a fugitive from justice."

"Now to come to Mitchell's story," continued Mr. Greer. "No statement was made by Doughty during the long train trip, according to Mitchell, until they got to Windsor and I think we can accept Mitchell's story as true. Mitchell states that Doughty refused to allow anything to be put in the statement about his sister or to incriminate any other person. If you read the statement you will see that is exactly what did happen. Doughty signs a statement saying he put the bonds in a safety-deposit box himself. That was untrue, and was done to protect the sister to whom he gave the bonds."

In conclusion, Mr. Greer declared that Doughty had gone to the safety-deposit box and in a "three-minute grab" had taken the bonds and then both he and his relatives had failed to take any reasonable steps later to return the bonds to the proper authorities. "He has by his conduct brought the whole family into the mess they are now in," he said, ending an address of one hour and twenty minutes.

Mr. Hellmuth, in opening his speech for the defence, drew a parallel from the crown counsel's address to the time when warfare was carried on with poisoned weapons, and to the time of the Boer War when wells were poisoned.

"There is an indictment of a family—the indictment of sister and brother, or perhaps of sisters and brother.

"The police are out for blood and they feel they will bear

114

the contempt of the community unless they can get John Doughty's head.

"The bonds are here—not a coupon cut off. The bonds are restored by this wicked family who have not attempted to cash one single bond or coupon.

"Nothing has been converted to Doughty's use.

"Unless he is guilty of theft, his moral actions otherwise are not before you," said Mr. Hellmuth.

"Anyone who, like my friend the crown attorney, has been prosecuting for so many years cannot help but press for a conviction when he gets before a jury," he declared.

Defence counsel read with emphasis the clause of the Criminal Code of Canada which deals with the use of Power of Attorney, and stressed the point that there must have been some conversion of these bonds or misuse of them to constitute an offence.

"I am not for one moment saying John Doughty was justified in taking the bonds out to present to Mr. Small and saying, 'Don't you intend to make me a present of some of them?' But, if he never fraudulently converted them to his own use, there is no theft.

"I may do a thousand foolish things, a thousand stupid things, but these are not necessarily criminal offences.

"Mr. Mitchell has failed utterly to show that Doughty stole the bonds or had any intent to steal them. It is my client's belief that the bonds were returned to a safety-deposit box and that Jeannie had the key and Jeannie was an honest woman.

"On his return when he first had a chance to speak to Jeannie, he asked her if she had the key to the deposit box and she told them she had no key . . . there never was a key. Doughty was surprised that the bonds had never been in a safety-deposit box and then asked his sister if all the bonds were accounted for. He seemed concerned about that.

"There is not the slightest suggestion of any pledge, sale or disposition of this property, or the conversion of it to Doughty's use.

"Theft is the taking of something fraudulently with intent to deprive the owner, but however foolish Doughty might have been, he was not guilty under the statute.

"A.J. Small or his estate has not lost a cent by Doughty's conduct," said Mr. Hellmuth.

"The Crown felt that it could not secure a conviction on this evidence, so it suggested in the evidence that John Doughty knew something of the disappearance of A.J. Small. It is the method of trying to get a conviction on one crime by suggesting another. That is a vile practice, and fortunately that is not British justice. It is not the way trials are conducted or should be conducted.

"John Doughty knows no more of Small's whereabouts than do you or I," he declared.

Following Hellmuth's impassioned request to the jury to find his client not guilty of theft, Judge Denton made a brief "charge" to the jury, reading with slow deliberateness the section of the Criminal Code concerning theft—the taking of another's property.

He did not summarize the testimony, telling the twelve men that he had watched them carefully during the two-day trial and he considered that they were intent listeners and displayed the reactions of reasonable and intelligent men.

The verdict, after an hour's deliberation, was to be expected: Guilty.

Doughty showed no emotion. He smiled wanly when the press group thundered from the courtroom. He looked around for Jeannie but she had disappeared just before the verdict, as if anticipating the result. His other sister, Mrs. Lovatt, was weeping.

Mr. Hellmuth asked the judge if he would reserve sentencing the defendant as it was his intention to file an appeal based on the admission of improper evidence. He thought that the court had no right to permit the introduction of evidence concerning Doughty's mental state and his "ramblings about theft" and "kidnapping and other dire deeds," when he was charged only with theft.

"I will hear your arguments on April 4th," said the judge, and left the bench. Doughty was taken by a guard to the Don Jail to await the appeal. He was denied bail.

When the "leave to appeal" was finally heard by Judge Denton, the defence lost its case. The judge explained that Doughty was charged only with theft and had admitted in a police statement to having taken the bonds. "That should be a prima facie case," said the judge as he sentenced Doughty to five years in penitentiary.

"That is a most unusual and cruel sentence," commented Mr. Hellmuth, his voice choked with emotion. "Nothing was really stolen, he gave the bonds up, his family tried to return them on a number of occasions. Without offending your honour, I have the feeling that my client has been tried for the disappearance of Small."

Don't be impertinent, Mr. Hellmuth," snapped the judge. He bowed to counsel who were present and left the bench.

Chapter Eleven

The excitement of John Doughty's apprehension and trial temporarily removed the sting of public and newspaper criticism which the Toronto and Provincial police had suffered for their failure to find some trace of Ambrose Small.

But the Small case was still hot news, and newsmen were critical of the way that police had handled the investigation right from the start. Talking with private detectives from the United States, newsmen realized that many essential ingredients necessary to modern crime investigation had been overlooked. No search of the furnace room of the Grand Opera House had ever been ordered. If Small had been battered over the head, surely there must have been traces of splattered blood in the room. Where was the shovel that was said to have been used to batter Small? Wouldn't there have been hair or flesh on such a shovel? Had the furnace been emptied of ashes and diligently searched for bone fragments?

Mitchell's explanation for these shortcomings was that Small was presumed to have run away or to be suffering from amnesia and now, a year and a half after the disappearance, all possible clues to murder had long since disappeared.

Newsmen asked Mitchell why he had dug up so much ground in Rosedale Ravine, if he thought at the time that Small had walked away from his wife to start a new life elsewhere. Mitchell explained that the digging was continuing because some of his clairvoyant friends insisted that Small had been murdered and buried in the ravine, while others thought that he would soon turn up somewhere in the world. Trying to please the occult wisdom was difficult, Mitchell admitted.

But he was a man dedicated to the case and would not give up the search. A body washed up on the Toronto beaches would bring him to the scene looking for hammertoes. A skeleton turned up at Collingwood, Ontario, more than a hundred miles from Toronto, but dental work showed the body to be that of a female missing from Brantford. The decomposed and bloated body of a man about Small's build and dressed in a tuxedo was found floating in the middle of Lake Ontario by a yachting party. The smelly body was dragged to Toronto and again Mitchell was on the scene with a press following. The man was identified as a Rochester suicide. The case might have died down at this time except for Theresa, who announced that Small's millions would be willed by her to the Catholic Church. This jolted Protestant Toronto like an earthquake and the pendulum of suspicion turned in the direction of Theresa Small.

Reporter Gordon Hogarth of the *Toronto Telegram* spotted Theresa attending a St. Michael's Cathedral mass, several days after this announcement in the press, and he asked her if it was true that she was leaving Small's fortune to the Church. She told him that it was, and as soon as the estate was free of the courts, his millions would be donated to the Order of the Sisters of Service and several other Catholic institutions.

When Hogarth remarked that Small was a Protestant, Theresa turned her back and entered her limousine. Hogarth then raced to the office of Frank Regan, the attorney assisting in legal work of the estate, and asked why the sisters of Ambrose—Florence and Gertrude—were not sharing in the brother's riches. Regan informed the reporter that Theresa had planned to leave a substantial amount to the two women even though the entire estate had been willed to her with no one else included. The will had been written by Small and witnessed in 1903, but a request by Small asked that the sisters be provided with the lifetime interest of $100,000.

Florence and Gertrude Small immediately challenged Theresa in the daily press by charging there had been another will made in 1917 or 1918, in which they were to share in the estate. They asked the provincial authorities to hold a court of inquiry. It would take fourteen years for this request to be granted.

During the summer of 1922, the federal government released to Mrs. Small some $800,000 of the estate and an allowance of $30,000 annually for living expenses until the entire estate had been cleared for succession duties. The sisters, Florence and Gertrude, charged they had been "officially" sentenced to starvation by the government and were left nothing of the estate, despite the fact that Ambrose had taken care of them since they were youngsters.

In September the sisters filed a claim against the estate asking for $200 a month and $7,000 in arrears that had not been paid to them since Small's disappearance. On November 11, following the Armistice Services before the Toronto City Hall, this claim was heard by Chief Justice R.M. Meredith of the Ontario Supreme Court. He arbitrarily set aside the orders of the government, and Theresa was forced to pay the $800,000 back into the estate as well as interest on that amount "until you have proven your right by established legal procedures."

Toronto reacted with glee. Mayor Tommy Church, who rode in Toronto's annual Orange Parade on July 12 as Grand Marshal and "King Billy," praised the court for its decision. He thought that police investigation should continue with all the fever of a new case. If the continuing investigation failed to turn up Small, at least Theresa would not get any money from the estate.

During this interim, the Loyal Orange Lodge gathered its strength to stop the Small estate from ending in the coffers of the Catholic Church. The Orangemen were supported wholeheartedly by the Sons of England, the Empire Club of Toronto, the Canadian Club, the Military Institute, the Church of England in Canada, and a host of other lodges, fraternal orders and Protestant churches with a combined power to influence all the newspapers, all government representatives and the very courts of justice.

There were no holds barred. Like waves of windblown confetti, pamphlets reminiscent of the broadsides of the seventeenth century swept over the streets of Toronto, and instead of finding their ultimate destination in the waste cans, they established a gutter library in the homes of the city residents. These underground sheets of trash and blasphemous libel branded Theresa Small a murderess and charged that she conspired with the Catholic Church and its priests to murder her husband so that the Church would get his millions. The propaganda was vicious. Yet, it was accepted. Theresa was forced to retire into the shadows of Glen Road and became a recluse, abandoning her friends, her clubs, and her social activities. Only the priests and nuns were constantly in her home, and they were not overlooked by the press.

The pressure upon the Toronto Police Department and the Ontario Provincial Police was enormous. The populace, like subscribers to a Roman Circus, wanted the disappearance of Ambrose Small linked to Theresa. There was a motive—money for her church, as well as evidence that Ambrose was a playboy with at least one mistress in the city. Yelling for Theresa's head were Florence and Gertrude and with banners flying they were familiar loudmouths in the newspaper offices of the downtown dailies.

Into this highly charged blasphemous atmosphere, on the eve of religious strife in the city, crashed an unsavoury character who was to keep the Small case alive for many more years.

He was described by police of two continents with glowing epithets such as: unscrupulous, immoral, uncouth, an unmitigated congenital liar, master of innuendo and half-truth, rabble-rouser, villain, and thief. He was at one time familiar to Liverpool and London police. Alberta Provincial Police held a warrant for his arrest and Scotland Yard had a dossier on him a yard long. At the height of the demoniac vilification of Theresa Small, he joined the fray and only missed being Mayor of Toronto by a handful of votes, and that was attributed to the fact that he was in jail at the time of the campaign.

His name was Patrick Sullivan.

Although his name sounded Irish and perhaps even Catholic, he was neither. Still, he was all things to all men and would do anything for money as long as it did not involve manual labour or regular hours of work. He went so far as to sleep with the ugly Small sisters in the raging battle to win money from the Small estate.

But first, and before the Alberta warrant had caught up with him in Toronto, Sullivan announced to the Toronto press that he was a well-known European criminologist and might be interested in solving the case if Theresa would want him. He thought he could solve the disappearance with fingerprints.

Sullivan was tall and slim with a narrow face and dark haunting eyes. He sported a thin mustache and appeared to be the embodiment of an illustrator's idea of a Mississippi gambler. His rapier-sharp mind immediately caught the Toronto picture as he stepped from a boxcar in the Grand Trunk yards. More than two million dollars was at stake and the first move, as he saw it, was to woo Theresa. He would start by being a criminologist.

But Theresa disliked him instantly, and she had him ejected from her Glen Road mansion. "I'll get you for this," he hissed. And he did.

He wooed and won Florence and Gertrude Small, together. He was parading around Toronto with a sister on each
arm and described himself as a "family adviser for justice."

His plan of action was to get the Small millions for Florence
and Gertrude, and this could only be accomplished by charging Theresa with murder or charging her with conspiring with
the Catholic Church to slay her husband. But first he had to call
Austin Mitchell a numskull and sow the seed of dissension in
the Toronto police and in the local political structure. He
accomplished this task with a series of underground pamphlets
claiming that Mitchell was in the pay of Theresa and that the
two of them had contrived to bungle the legitimate efforts of
other investigators.

Having sown these words, he came forth with the sisters,
charging that a second will had been destroyed by Theresa;
that the cellar in the Glen Road home had not been dug up
even after a maid had seen Theresa saying her beads over a spot
in the cellar floor; that the Grand Opera basement had not
been excavated; and that the Rosedale Ravine had not been
turned over in the proper spots, closer to the Small home.

These items were reported in the press with front-page
banners and brought some action. Mitchell and Hammond
with a squad of officers dug up the furnace room of the Opera
House and found nothing. Next, they descended on Glen Road
and were astounded at the layout of the mansion.

Over Theresa's protests, Mitchell, apologetic and visibly
upset, gave the signal to six policemen to start chopping into
the basement floors, while he and Hammond made a tour of
the premises, looking into sixteen rooms on three floors, more
in curiosity and awe than in the manner of detectives searching
for clues. One of the accompanying constables, however, made
sketches of the tour. Fifty-one Glen Road was entered by a
small oak-panelled vestibule, in which were located a large
wall mirror and a coat rack. A massive oak door with stained

glass in the upper half led into the main hallway which travelled some fifteen feet to a rotunda of oak and plaster with a magnificent crystal chandelier sparkling from the heavy chain in the very centre of this circular roundabout.

From the rotunda, all rooms on the first floor were connected by oaken doors, massive and brooding in the dim pink light of stained glass from a landing on the staircase. The mansion faced due west. The northwest room was the music room, linked by the oaken door to the rotunda and to the large front veranda by two French doors. It was a conservative room with heavy marble statuary and two large sombre paintings, all of which had been purchased in Italy by Theresa. She confided to Mitchell that she rarely used the music room after Amby's disappearance. A white sheet laid neatly over the outlines of a grand piano provided the room with the appearance of a tomb, old and neglected, and guarded by the sculptured ghosts of other years, musty and with a faint fragrance of lavender from some dried flowers on the mantel.

The southwest room was the living room, massive in size with thick burgundy drapes that cloaked out the light from the west. Two stained-glass windows were high on the south wall, embracing a great fireplace of brick and panelled oak. These windows showed Theresa's captivation by the colour pink. Drapes were mostly in deep blood-reds. The room was not lavishly furnished; it contained a large sofa, two chairs of the Georgian period and a small writing-desk of great antiquity. The room, she pointed out, was never used, except during past periods of social entertainment, which over the first decade of the couple's married life had been frequent and colourful.

To the southeast of the rotunda was the formal dining room where Mitchell, in December 1919, had sipped tea with Theresa when she asked him not to inform the newspapers of Amby's disappearance. Hammond looked briefly at the lavish use of oak and textured burgundy wallpaper, and then peeked into the kitchen at the northeast section. The constable noted that a staircase led from the north side of the rotunda to the basement and to a side doorway. There was also a very narrow set of steps upward from this stairway and Theresa explained this was the passageway for the servants, to their quarters on the third storey. From the neat white kitchen, a stairway led downward to a pantry landing and then doubled back and downward into the basement. Access to the rear yard was through a doorway at the pantry level of the staircase, a dark unfriendly area without any window light.

The second floor, connected to the first by a curved staircase on the south side, contained a second rotunda, directly above the first but slightly smaller in size and similarly illuminated from the dull pink of the stained-glass windows of the stairway landing. A sculptured brass ceiling fixture provided a discreet glow, reflected from the gold-embossed ceiling.

The northwest room over the downstairs music room was Theresa's sewing room. It was bright and cheerful and it was evident that this was the room in which she entertained her friends from the convent as well as the priests who were often in the house. It had a mahogany serving table, a number of high-back mahogany chairs and several pieces of art and sculpture. On this occasion, Hammond and Mitchell were served tea in this room by a weeping Theresa who was angered and humiliated by the arrival of the police and the dull and distant pounding that was taking place in the basement.

The southwest room was also bright and was Theresa's bedroom, containing a double bed, two chairs, a small white writing-desk, white curtains, and an unused fireplace with the stained glass windows of pink on either side. Heavy drapes were pulled aside and Glen Road and the lovely trees of Rosedale could be seen westward of the mansion.

The southeast room, overlooking the rear yard and directly over the dining room, was the one-time retreat of Ambrose

Small. A massive desk, with a large onyx pen set atop of it, dominated the room by its position directly in front of the large rear window. Theresa opened the shades. The bed was of medium size and two chairs in brown leather filled up the panelled space. A desk lamp over some books on the desk was cast in bronze and complemented the greatness of the desk. A bureau clung to the north wall next to a doorway that led into a closet and thence into the bathroom which took the northeast space of the second floor.

The officers saw nothing significant in their perusal of Ambrose's room. There was a watch on the desk. Theresa said it was under her husband's pillow the morning after he failed to return home. Police thought there was no significance in that. Business and personal papers had long since been removed from the desk. Small's black suits and dress shirts were missing from the sombre closet. Theresa had given them to Percy Small, her nephew. The bathroom was large and all in white tile with a huge pedestal sink and a massive white bathtub which Ambrose had once boasted was the largest tub in all of Toronto. When the home was planned, Ambrose permitted Theresa to approve the layout of rooms and their sizes but the bathroom was his and he ordered the largest tub he could find. It was an ambition that went back to his drab boyhood days when he was forced to wash in a wooden tub.

The third floor contained three small attic-type rooms, two for the maids and one for the chauffeur. There was also a bathroom with toilet, tub and sink.

The basement of 51 Glen Road was the area of most importance to the police. It was divided into four parts. The northeast corner was a clothes-washing room with an ironing board, a washing machine and deep concrete sinks. The floor was in grey tile. The door from the rear of this room led to the pantry landing and to the kitchen and also to the outside where a stoop was in evidence for hanging out the family wash.

The southeast room was a storage room and was sometimes utilized to hang washing on clotheslines on wet days. Some old furniture was stored here.

The northwest room, directly under the music room, was the furnace room and it was from this room that the heavy sounds of pounding were emanating. The room was small and almost completely filled by a steam boiler with twin loading doors. Clinkers of coal were piled in a narrow room to the side. To the front of this room was the coal room with a shute leading to the outside. It was filled with a fresh supply of hard coal.

Constables had broken the cement floor in front of the furnace doors, near the doorway, but it was obvious that the cement was original and the brown clay earth below was damp and untouched. Mitchell ordered the cement to be relaid and the floor painted in dull red.

The southwest room, directly under the living room, provided a mild shock to Hammond and Mitchell and drew forth exclamations of wonder from the constables. It was a shrine, Theresa's private shrine, and candles glowed in the semi-darkness, lending an eerie atmosphere to the tomblike room, where the ceiling was eight feet in height and a lone window on the south provided the only outside illumination.

This was the shrine where Theresa prayed before the altar of Flemish lace and heavy brass candles. A white bible lay open on the altar. A gold cord, twisted and tasselled, kept the pages apart. On the wall above the altar was a statue of the Virgin. On the right wall, which was the north wall, was an Italian painting of the Bleeding Heart, and hand-carved crucifixes broke the shadows along the other walls. The floor was heavily carpeted in Orientals and a tapestry covered the east wall by the entranceway.

Earlier, a maid had told police that Ambrose had never seen the shrine and had refused to go near it. He never went into the cellar for any reason. Infuriated from time to time with the parade of priests and nuns, he insisted the processions use the side door and enter the shrine in that manner, without crowding onto the front veranda in full view of his neighbours, some of whom were his Protestant friends and cronies.

Mitchell ordered the rugs rolled back while he made an examination of the floor. It was cement and painted grey. There was a drain plug at the south side under the window. The cement was rough and uneven but a decision was made at this time not to chop the floor. This decision would someday fall heavily on Mitchell's shoulders.

Following the inspection, Mitchell promised Theresa he would continue his investigation with all the vigour at his command. Before returning to headquarters, the group walked through the backyard, resplendent in autumn leaves from the great oaks. There was nothing significant found in the two-car garage or in the attic above the garage. It was noted that the front veranda was formed by concrete and over the scene looked two great Grecian urns of concrete and bronze, reflecting the late afternoon sun as did the French windows to the left and the bay windows of the downstairs living room to the right.

If the solution to the mystery of Small's disappearance lay at 51 Glen Road, the officers failed to find it. There were those who felt the probe should have gone much deeper—below all the basement floors.

Chapter Twelve

Patrick Sullivan was undaunted. He joined the Orange Lodge and made certain he was seen in various Protestant churches in Toronto with the sisters on his arms. When the Alberta Provincial Police heard that Sullivan was in Toronto, a warrant was telegraphed for his immediate arrest.

When the matter was brought to Mitchell for discussion, he told Guthrie it was a good chance for them to get Sullivan off their backs. They asked for more details before making their move. From Alberta came the strange case of Sullivan.

Apparently he was born in London in 1888. At least Scotland Yard believed that was the city where he was born, although they were never sure. He flitted from city to city on the Continent with two purposes in life; to make money illegally, and to sexually conquer as many women as he could. Uppermost in his mind was someday to unite both goals, money and sex in one grand package.

Sometime around 1920 he arrived in Halifax in the steerage after a hasty retreat from Liverpool where police almost caught him at the dockside. They had numerous charges of fraud against him. With a forged passport, he was admitted to Canada as a "private investigator" and he headed by slow freight to Edmonton.

He applied to the Alberta Provincial Police in Edmonton

for a position. He told them he was a fingerprint expert, a well-known criminologist in England and a former detective with Scotland Yard. He was immediately hired. Apparently, his credentials were never checked. It was a long way from Edmonton to London. And besides, Sullivan started into his new position with great vigour in tracking down bootleggers and prostitutes. He became a familiar figure in the sleezier outskirts of town.

Sullivan's ability to sniff out crime brought considerable praise from his superiors and he was chosen to lead an investigative team into the wilderness of the Peace River District to solve the disappearance of a woodcutter by the name of William Doherty. Several other woodcutters had vanished in the same district.

His success may have been pure luck or it may have been that he kept his eyes on all Wanted bulletins coming into the headquarters of the Alberta Provincial Police. In any event, he came upon the name of Mrs. William Doherty of Denver, Colorado. She was wanted for attempted murder and was on the ten-most-wanted list of that State.

The William Doherty missing in the Peace River District and the name of Mrs. William Doherty, missing from Denver, rang a bell. Why not? thought Sullivan. If she is wanted for trying to kill in one place and her husband and other men are missing in another, why not the same woman? After all, the Peace River wilderness was not unlike Colorado.

Sullivan wired for more information. Denver informed him that Mrs. Doherty, a rather attractive woman in her midtwenties, known in Colorado as Sylvia Brown, was a former mental patient, with a penitentiary record as well. She was wanted for attempting to poison the family of William Doherty, his ex-wife (if she was ex at that time), his mother, father and three or perhaps four children. Denver police believed that

Doherty was unaware of the attempted mass murder as he had left Colorado for other lumber camps.

Patrick Sullivan and two other officers started on their way northwest, into the land of silence and mountain wilderness.

Within a week they located the Doherty cabin but there was no William and only a weepy Sylvia. Yes, she told Patrick Sullivan, as they shared the same bed, she had killed her husband with an axe, and had poisoned his family in Denver because she wanted Doherty for herself. He had managed to get a contract to mark timber for winter cutting in the Peace River District and the two decided to go it alone. When he began to brood over his family, she axed him.

It took three nights of wild sex in the only bunk in the cabin for Sullivan to get the details of Sylvia's crimes.

"I would do anything for love," she purred into his ear, and Sullivan led her back to civilization after digging up Doherty's remains and reburying them on a pine ridge near the lonely cabin.

However, Sullivan told the other officers that Sylvia's hatcheting her husband was in self-defence after he had gone berserk in the wilderness and had tried to kill her. In Edmonton, Sullivan was hailed a hero by the senior officers of the force but he was fired the next day when they learned he had slept with the wanted woman.

"That's no way to get a confession," snapped the district magistrate. Sylvia was shipped back to Denver and the Peace River episode was dropped.

Collecting his back pay, Patrick Sullivan bought a gallon of rye, hired two prostitutes from a nearby bordello where he was a familiar figure, and headed to a hotel in town. The noise of the three-ring party caused problems for the hotel and the police were called. Sullivan was charged with drunken and disorderly conduct and was released on bail of twenty-five dollars to make his appearance before a magistrate in seven days.

That was not for Sullivan. He returned to the hotel, packed his few belongings and headed for the railroad yards. He hopped a freight train and landed in Toronto ten days later. The first thing that caught his roving eyes was a front-page story in the Toronto *Telegram* concerning the Small investigation and a feature story on the lonely Theresa Small. He called Theresa and told her he was a fingerprint expert.

Sullivan's background was dispatched to Mitchell by the Commissioner of Alberta Provincial Police. Mitchell decided to grab Sullivan and book him for the misdemeanour in Alberta.

"What are you going to do—pay my way back to Alberta?" sneered Sullivan, as Mitchell waved the warrant before his face.

Mitchell hadn't thought of that. A wired request to Edmonton for the rail fare for Sullivan was promptly turned down. Mitchell now realized that Patrick Sullivan would be throwing barbs at him. The newspapers paid more attention to Sullivan and his theory of the Small case than they did to all his investigations.

Sullivan started a Toronto tabloid newspaper, called the *Statesman*, with money from the Orange Lodge and from other sources. It was a weekly dedicated to Theresa and the Catholic Church. That this rag of innuendo, half-truths and outright lies, with diabolically retouched photographs, could have lasted as long as it did in a city known as Toronto the Good was an indication of the power of the Orange Lodge and the bitterness in the city against Theresa and her church.

Superimposed photographs on the front page of the *Statesman* showed Theresa naked on her bed having intercourse with a priest.

Toronto rocked with glee at the shocking photographs and

at trumped-up lies that Theresa also had personal relations with the Italian Vice-Consul in Toronto, as well as a number of prominent Catholics. She was in seclusion but knew of the onslaught on her moral character. Her lawyers seemed to be powerless to stop the libel.

At the Brunswick Avenue home of the two Small sisters, Sullivan was playing an adroit game of holding their affection without creating jealousy. He took Florence to a hotel in Kitchener where they registered as man and wife. He took Gertrude to Niagara Falls, also registering as man and wife.

And, as in a dark scene from Macbeth, the three plotted the downfall of Theresa Small so that Ambrose's millions would legally be theirs. They drew up a step-by-step program to meet their goal by having courts fighting courts, lawyers fighting and blackening other lawyers, churches striving against churches, governments fighting governments, and all the while linking the Catholic Church to blood money and connecting Theresa and her entire family to murder.

But Sullivan could not proceed any deeper at that precise moment for he did not have access to all the investigations. Hammond wouldn't speak to him and Mitchell was furious. Then Sullivan, with all the guile of a ferret playing with a chipmunk, approached Mitchell with the idea that clairvoyance might be the way to solve the case; he won a friend and the two began working together, from Gypsy parlours to crystal-ball gazers, Sullivan biding his time.

When Sullivan tired of the game he told Mitchell he had to know every detail of the case in order to get all the spirits in the right mood. Mitchell finally agreed. He had two files on the case, one for show and the other his private file. Even Hammond never knew of the latter.

Now Sullivan had that file, and he found the way to snare Theresa Small. The slice of evidence that Mitchell had kept secret was a sworn statement from Mrs. Mary Quigley of 94

133

Gould Street, a cleaning woman, that she saw a notice posted in the Convent of the Precious Blood on St. Joseph Street "requesting prayers for the repose of the soul of Ambrose J. Small."

The writing was in red and Mrs. Quigley swore she saw the notice before Small's disappearance was reported in the Toronto newspapers.

Patrick Sullivan's eyes bulged.

Did someone know that Small was dead before his disappearance was reported?

Who in the Catholic Church with access to the convent would know of such a thing?

Sullivan continued deeper into the secret files of Mitchell.

He found a statement by Catherine Dunn, who said she found Small's key and watch under his pillow but her statement gave the date as December 2, the day that Small went to his office earlier than usual.

To the first revelation was attached the following note: "Make inquiries at the convent to ascertain if there was any truth in the statement that notices were published by Mrs. Small shortly after the disappearance of Ambrose Small."

"Notices," gulped Sullivan. "What have we here, more than one?"

Next he found evidence that Theresa Small had produced a watch on December 19, the one which she said the maid found under the pillow. But she did not mention a key when she subsequently turned over the watch to Mitchell, who gave it back to her.

There was a mention that Mitchell or Hammond talked with Sisters Shank and Guest at the Sisters of Service convent across the street from the Small residence, but no mention was on file about the purpose of the interview.

Quiet investigation of the posting of a notice "in blood"

received an answer from a Toronto priest, that "the Convent of the Sisters of the Precious Blood, where the notice was posted requesting prayers for the soul of Ambrose Small, would not be at all accessible to laymen but was a cloistered convent and the bulletin board was not in any part of the convent to which the public had access."

In any event, Sullivan managed to leak this information to the press and the headlines re-opened the case again. Who posted the notices? Who had known or believed that Small was dead, before the news of his disappearance was published in January 1920?

Another report on the posting of the notices carried this statement: "As to the Sisters of St. Joseph, Mother Victoria was interviewed and she recalls a notice being posted in the usual form for a request for prayers for the intention of Mrs. Small.

"At the Convent of the Precious Blood, Mother Immaculate states that certain notices for request for prayers are posted on a board close to the Chapel which is in the cloistered area. No person except the cloistered Nuns, from that or some other convent, would have access to this area. . . . this Nun has only a vague recollection of the contents of this notice."

A detective's report on another date revealed the following: "I interviewed Mother Victoria at the Sisters of St. Joseph and she advised me that she was one of the Nuns in the Convent at the time of A.J. Small's disappearance. She stated that the invariable rule for requesting prayers was that someone should phone or call personally and give their name and the purpose for which the prayers were to be made and that one of the Sisters would then type on a sheet of paper: 'Prayers are requested for the intentions of . . .' But this paper never revealed the intentions for which the prayers were made. Mother Victoria does recollect that Sister Angela, who was a great friend of Mrs. Small and who is now dead, told her that

Mrs. Small had requested prayers some time in the latter part of 1919 or the early part of 1920. Mother Victoria does not remember anything else about it."

In the course of the next few days, Patrick Sullivan learned that there were exceptions to the rule that kept the cloistered areas of the convents from lay persons. He discovered that doctors, nurses, dentists, eletricians, plumbers and cleaning women were permitted in cloistered areas of all the convents.

"Why not Theresa Small?" he asked. "She was the chief benefactress . . . surely she had more right in the cloistered areas than some cleaning woman."

Probing deeper, with the help of his Orange Lodge friends, Sullivan learned that the Attorney General of Ontario's office had a file on the Small case and in that file was a statement concerning the posting of notices in the convents for the "repose of Small's soul."

He informed the Toronto newspapers and the commotion that followed revived the daily headlines. Theresa Small asked her attorney Frank Hughes to go before the courts immediately and have the will "proved" as well as "certain other affidavits." This issue was heard by Justice Coatsworth of the Supreme Court of Ontario who refused the application.

The decision brought an immediate appeal to the Appeal Court of Ontario, and on January 5, 1924, Coatsworth's order was declared invalid and Ambrose Small legally dead. With this decision, application was made for probate but Gertrude and Florence, with Sullivan at their side, opposed the application and the entire proceedings moved into the Supreme Court of Ontario for a decision concerning the original Will dated September 6, 1903, and other matters pertaining to the estate.

After lengthy and bitter court battles between prides of lawyers, the Supreme Court, bound by the order that Small was legally dead, awarded Theresa the entire estate, found the 1903 Will legal, but placed a proviso on the estate that Theresa pay into the Court a hundred thousand dollars from which the Small sisters would receive interest for the rest of their lives.

On April 24, 1924, Theresa agreed to this proviso. She had intended to do exactly this in the first place. The newsmen at the court asked Frank Hughes what would happen to the $100,000 after the last sister was dead and he replied that the principal would likewise be willed to the Catholic Church with the rest of Theresa's estate.

This statement received considerable publicity in the Toronto press and made Sullivan and the sisters and the Orange Lodge more determined than ever to link Theresa to the disappearance of Small and in that way upset the validity of her own will. But the investigation by Sullivan did not gain much momentum because the newspapers were tiring of the Small case. Other exciting things were taking place at this time. One of them was the advent of the radio and families were gathering nightly in their living rooms to listen to faraway music and dramatic voices that kept them pinned to earphones and radio speakers far into the night.

But the ghost of Ambrose Small refused to give up.

In late 1926, the Toronto *Star* received a collect call from Waupun, Wisconsin, a village lying some twenty miles from Fond du Lac. At first, the reporter who answered the phone refused to accept the collect call but when the party on the other end of the line said that he was Ambrose Small and had just "escaped," the reporter yelled for his City Editor and the two accepted the call.

"I am Ambrose Small," said the voice. "I am calling from a pay station in Waupun and I'll stay here until you save me."

"Where have you been?" asked the excited reporter.

"They locked me in a nuthouse here in December, 1919 . . . I have just managed to escape . . . they know me by the name of Charles Churchill . . . save me. I'll wait."

The *Star* called Mitchell and also placed a call to the

Chicago *Tribune*, with which the *Star* had an alliance on news coverage, and asked them to investigate the call.

Mitchell rushed to Glen Road. The *Tribune* phoned Fond du Lac and confirmed that an inmate by the name of Churchill had escaped. A country-wide search was in progress.

Mitchell told Theresa of the strange call. He had been provided with the phone number by the *Star* and, with Theresa at his side, Mitchell called the number in Waupun.

"Are you Ambrose Small?" asked Mitchell.

"Yes," replied the voice.

"How did you get to Waupun, wherever that is?"

"I was kidnapped in Toronto and brought here in December 1919 . . . this is the first time I have managed to get loose. . . . I have been behind bars . . . locked up . . . where is my wife?"

Theresa picked up the phone, uncertain what to expect. But Mitchell was dancing around. "It's him, it's him!" he said to an incredulous Josephine who was present at the conversation.

"This is Theresa," she said softly into the mouthpiece. She nodded her head several times without speaking and then, swaying as if on the verge of losing consciousness, she turned to Mitchell and exclaimed: "It can't be . . . but it sounds like my Amby."

Mitchell and his following of reporters made an immediate rush to buy train tickets. Chicago *Tribune* reporters, with a photograph of Small in their possession, drove through the night and found the person who had made the call in a pay booth, exactly where he had told the *Star* he could be found.

A reporter, placing the photo of Small against this man, exclaimed: "It's him . . . it's Ambrose Small."

News of the discovery broke like a bombshell. The theatre magnate was alive! Theresa called her personal physician and asked him to leave at once for Wisconsin. Mitchell was on the way by train with a squad of reporters.

"I was right," beamed Mitchell, and a photo of him appeared in the dailies with a big smile on his face.

But back in Waupun, authorities of the Wisconsin Asylum for the Insane reached the escapee before Mitchell and hauled him back to the institution. The District Attorney of Fond du Lac ordered an immediate investigation. Department sleuths found that Churchill was the wrong age—he was twenty years younger than Small would now have been. Not only that, but he had spent most of his life in the Waupun institution. His room was piled high with newspaper and magazine articles on the Small case. An avid reader, he had digested all the details, dates, names and locations, and when at last he made his escape he was ready to take Small's place.

Chapter Thirteen

"What about the bloody writing asking for prayers posted in the convents?" shouted Patrick Sullivan from a vantage point on the steps of a downtown Toronto church. Florence and Gertrude were at his side. He was using church steps and the concrete bases of statues in Toronto parks to attract crowds to keep the Small investigation alive.

Shouting and gesticulating, he was a familiar figure in all districts of the city and when he would suggest that Theresa and her Catholic priests be jailed for murder, the crowds went wild with glee. At one period, prior to these outbursts, Sullivan most often included Mitchell and the Toronto police force in his fiery vilifications, but since he had been given access to the private files he was more cautious. He had been forced to stop publication of the *Statesman* because of threats of a suit for libel by Theresa Small and for blasphemous libel by the Church. He therefore bided his time waiting for the threats to subside and Austin Mitchell unknowingly provided a distracting interval.

Mitchell had been reading glowing reports from Los Angeles, New York City, Chicago and Regina, about Dr. Maxmilian Langsner and his "thought process" for solving baffling crimes.

Said to be one of Vienna's most outstanding criminologists, Langsner had come to the United States and then to Western

Canada to assist police in tracking down a slippery murderer. In Saskatchewan, he used his "thought process" and turned up a man who was immediately charged, tried, and hanged. This provided Langsner with considerable publicity, particularly in Hollywood, where his type of mind-reading was less a novelty than a way of life.

Mitchell had gathered a number of news articles about Langsner and had gone so far as to call Regina to ascertain if the criminologist was as great as his publicity; he was assured that Langsner was a miracle man in crime investigation. Mitchell called Langsner, told him of the Small enigma, about which Langsner had already heard, and invited him to Toronto to solve the case.

Dr. Langsner agreed to come at once. Mitchell called the Toronto newspapers and Sullivan's stumping was momentarily forgotten. Small's disappearance was at last about to be solved.

The criminologist arrived at Toronto's Union Station with all the fanfare of a silent movie star. Scores of newsmen and photographers, curious crowds and Austin Mitchell welcomed the distinguished sleuth. Dr. Langsner was charming in his graciousness, chatted amiably with the press, told them his secrets would be their secrets and he would be ready to embark on the "thought process" in about seven days. He required this length of time to study all aspects of the Small case.

At the expense of the Toronto Police, he was provided with a suite in the King Edward Hotel. No one seemed to inquire why he needed a suite with "at least three bedrooms." He was accompanied by a number of hip-swinging young women, who followed him everywhere with adoring glances and starry-eyed devotion. Langsner referred to this covey as his "believers," and bellhops in the King Edward were at first surprised to hear giggles followed by screams and the sounds of beatings and sobbings coming from the suite each night. But when Langsner explained that he was conjuring a "thought process," no one investigated further.

On the day chosen by Langsner to conduct the "thought process," Mitchell paced the hallway with reporters outside Langsner's rooms. When the doctor finally dashed into the corridor he was breathless and perspiration flowed from his forehead, over his narrow face and into his thick beard. His black eyes were shining. His lips formed a smile, almost cynical, perfectly smug.

"I have conjured an astral vision with great difficulty," said Langsner over the noise of the scratching pencils of a score of reporters. "At first the vision was cloudy but gradually I saw the vision appear . . . Ambrose Small was kidnapped to Montreal . . . to a rooming house in the downtown part of the city . . . was murdered and his body was thrown into a furnace."

The announcement excited Montreal but fell with a dull thud in Toronto. Some newsmen, as well as Mitchell, thought that Langsner had automatically linked Doughty's trip to Montreal on the night of December 2 with the murder of Small. But where was the rooming house? Langsner didn't know.

Montreal police began an immediate search of the house where John Doughty had roomed during December of 1919. The landlady could not recall the number of roomers at that time and certainly not the comings and goings at the house. Examination of the coal-burning furnace turned up no clues.

Mitchell asked Langsner to try again. Perhaps the "astral vision" had settled over Montreal by mistake. Could he have it hover over Toronto?

Langsner said he would try, and buried himself behind locked doors with his followers.

Five days later and after consuming a mountain of steaks and onions, Langsner announced that he had relocated Small's astral vision. It was not in Montreal. It was in Toronto, all the time. Langsner had made a mistake in his vision of the city.

"Mr. Small is dead and is buried in a ravine someplace," he intoned. "I can see the ravine quite clearly and I will lead you there."

Followed by a crowd of newsmen, onlookers, and police, Langsner led the way to a spot in the Rosedale Ravine and since the place was less than half a mile from Small's Glen Road residence, Mitchell and the others were impressed.

"Dig in this vicinity," commanded Langsner, and everyone began to pitch in and stir up the clay and gravel of the ravine wilderness. While all the digging was in progress, Langsner had a second vision and he confided to Mitchell that he could see a pig farm in the vicinity of Rosedale. The vision was not investigated further.

Langsner disappeared from Toronto leaving a hefty bill for the police department.

Patrick Sullivan was ready to pounce again. He brought forth not only the *Statesman* but also another tabloid called *Thunderer*. Retouched photos of Theresa and a number of priests and nuns were so filthy that the police recoiled in horror. The issues now running on the press flatly charged Theresa and her church with murder but these issues never saw the city lights.

A squad of morality detectives raided the Sovereign Press where the tabloids were printed. They seized all copies of the newspapers, scattered the type and destroyed the engravings of the retouched photographs. Within minutes they arrested Sullivan and charged him with distributing obscene literature. While he was raging in the cells of the City Hall, further investigation of the publications by the crown attorney brought about another charge, one that was much more serious: criminal libel.

It was not until early January 1930 that a preliminary hearing forced Sullivan to stand trial before the Supreme Court of Ontario on both charges. By now, Small had been missing just over ten years but the case seemed as fresh as ever.

Evidence at his trial disclosed that all the writing in the tabloids had been accomplished by Sullivan alone. The photographers of the smut and the retouchers of the photos could not be located but the prosecutor told the court that Sullivan gathered prostitutes from the street corners, picked out those that resembled Theresa in some manner and then placed naked "priests," with their robes thrown nearby, into the sexy positions of chesterfield love-making.

"Overwhelming evidence," said Justice McEvoy, as he sentenced Sullivan to a year at hard labour. A second trial followed quickly on the charge of distributing obscene literature and now the Orange Lodge raised a cry of protest. Sullivan was being tried by Justice Daniel O'Connell, a noted Catholic jurist in Toronto.

But Toronto was tiring of Sullivan and of the Orange Lodge. The citizens had rather enjoyed the attacks on Theresa and her church but tampering with the courts of law was another matter. Justice O'Connell never commented about the attacks on his religion and sentenced Sullivan to an additional sixteen months in jail.

But Sullivan was not sent to prison. He was, instead, incarcerated in the Mimico Reformatory, ten miles west of Toronto, where most of the prisoners were overnight drunks, minor wife-beaters and alcoholics. Prisoners in this reformatory had a great deal of freedom on wide-open acres dedicated to farming and brick-making. Visitors were permitted every day, boxing matches were held at night in the gymnasium, and other activities kept the prisoners entertained. Sullivan enjoyed all the "open" privileges and more. From his office in the cell block he was permitted to campaign for the mayoralty of Toronto.

He was duly nominated by two members of the Orange Lodge, and from his cell he wrote the editorial copy for posters and pamphlets that swirled across the city. But being in jail deprived Sullivan of his great ability of rabble-rousing and his opponents were drawing increasing support. Sullivan lost the vote by a very narrow margin and there were many who believed that if he had been free to conduct meetings at the time of the race, he might have won the seat as the Chief Magistrate of Toronto.

A petition by the Citizens for Toronto, formed from certain church groups as well as from the Orange Lodge, circulated with thousands of signatures to have Sullivan released. On March 31, 1931, after serving only twelve months of the total of twenty-eight months, Sullivan was met at the reformatory gates by Florence and Gertrude and half a dozen newsmen. He swore to continue the investigation of the Small case with all the fervour and strength of his body. His declaration made only a paragraph in the Toronto dailies and the case simmered while Mitchell dug ground and Sullivan continued to plot.

Theresa Small died in her Glen Road home on October 14, 1935. Ill health caused by diabetes, as well as by the haunting events of the past sixteen years, left her bedridden and alone. All her friends, except those of the Church, had abandoned her.

At her bedside when she passed away were two priests and several nuns from the Sisters of Service, whom she loved so much and who had stood by her side through all the turmoil of bigotry. Toronto was not to know of her death until Wednesday, October 16, when a simple death announcement appeared in the obituary column of the Toronto *Star*.

The funeral service, held the next morning at Our Lady of Lourdes Roman Catholic Church on Sherbourne Street, was one of the largest in Ontario history and certainly the largest in the Catholic Church history in Canada. From all parts of the province and from Montreal and Quebec came devoted Catholics like pilgrims to a shrine. The people of Toronto, apparently realizing that some of the shame belonged to them, flocked to the church to pay their last respects to the greatest single benefactress the church had ever known.

More than a thousand persons, dignitaries of Toronto, members of the Provincial Legislature, Members of Parliament, and representatives of all the Toronto Diocese Catholic Orders participated in the High Requiem Mass. Thousands were turned away and special squads of police were on hand to keep the crowd behind the rope barriers. The service was one and a half hours in length and the final eulogy described Theresa as a "fine and noble woman."

Suffering in silence were the priests and nuns of the orders that Theresa had befriended: the Sisters of St. Joseph, the Sisters of Service, the Christian Brothers, the Fathers of the Redemptorist Order and the Sisters of the Precious Blood.

In the Sacristy were the Toronto Monsignors of her church and her confessors, Rev. Dean L. Hand and Rev. John Blair. In front of the casket before the High Altar were twenty pews for her relatives and old friends like Monsignor J. B. Dollard who sang the High Mass.

Farther back in the candle-decked church were other church orders and groups of one-time friends. There, sad in lonely contemplation, were the members of the Christian Mothers, the Altar Society and the Catholic Women's League. Supervisors of the Ladies of Loretta, the Catholic Infants' Home and the Little Sisters Misericorde of St. Mary's Hospital and the Glen Road Novitiate, as well as the ladies of the Henry Pellatt Chapter of the Imperial Order Daughters of the Empire, participated in the final rites.

There was no representation from the Orange Lodge, whose power had now waned. Patrick Sullivan and the Small sisters were not present. John Doughty, out of prison and operating a service station in East Toronto, was not seen, although reporters were watching for him.

After the funeral service, Theresa's hearse, preceded by Toronto Police motorcycles, moved north on Sherbourne Street, west on Bloor Street past the old Kormann home and north on Yonge Street to St. Michael's Cemetery on the hill. The pallbearers, James E. Day, K.C., W. T. Kernahan, J. P. Hynes, J.P. Mullen, W.L. Gray and H.T. Rosler carried the casket past the Kormann plot. She was buried in an unmarked grave which would soon be shared by her sister Josephine. To the curious who would later descend on the cemetery, no tombstone or animated bust would betray the whereabouts of Theresa Small's last resting place beneath the even turf.

Now that Theresa was gone, her will would be probated according to the law of Ontario, opening again the entire Small case, ensnarling lawyers, government investigators, Patrick Sullivan and the Small sisters. The explosions that now developed made the antics of the past sixteen years look like rank amateurism.

Theresa's will disclosed that she had kept her promise. The bulk of a two-million-dollar estate went to various Catholic Orders, with the Sisters of Service on Glen Road receiving most of the money. She left to her relatives one thousand dollars each. The highest single bequest was for $5,000 and this was paid to a niece, Mrs. E. W. Rush, who had been close to her until death.

Prodded by Sullivan, the Small sisters marched into court and presented a caveat—a legal manoeuvre to hold up the execution of the will. They charged that Theresa was guilty of Small's murder, that Toronto and Provincial police had fallen down on the job, that Small's chauffeur had never been questioned, nor had the maids in the Small household—all of whom had a story to tell.

The *Thunderer* mysteriously appeared again. The first re-issue of the smut organ asked why one of the Small maids had been committed to an insane asylum after Small's disappearance. Why was Theresa, on the night of Small's murder, praying in the basement with candles over a particular spot on the cellar floor, and who put the notices of "prayers for Small" in the two Toronto convents?

The clamour that followed these questions rose in a new crescendo, then Sullivan announced that a "confession" by Theresa had been left to the Small sisters to be opened after her death.

Austin Mitchell believed in first things first. He dug up the cellar again in the Glen Road home. He found nothing, only the evidence that the cellar had been dug up before. But the people of Toronto wanted more facts in the case before the money was paid into the Catholic Church, and it became necessary to conduct an official government probe of the entire affair from start to finish.

The highest criminal investigation authority in the Province of Ontario was the Attorney General's Department. In 1936, the Attorney General was the distinguished Arthur Roebuck, a gentleman of great talent and infinite patience, a superb lawyer and a quizzical individual, who with his narrow stooped shoulders, his wavy grey hair and a black ribbon hanging from his spectacles, commanded great admiration and respect. Roebuck was sometimes cautious in the extreme, but the mounting cry from the public for a full probe of the Small case after almost seventeen years of police investigation led him in only one direction. The case had to be continued but with precise avenues of investigation.

Roebuck sent a crack team of sleuths into the case. They were augmented by Pinkerton detectives, some of whom came from the United States to assist in the work. At the same time, the attorneys for the Small estate hired their own detectives to dig into the muck of years gone by without losing sight of the main quest, to prove that the "confession" now in Roebuck's hands was a fraud.

The reporters of the Toronto dailies dug up more information and better news features than the professional sleuths.

The first duty of police and medical legal teams was to prove that Theresa was sane until the time of her death. Her doctors said she was.

Another duty was to round up all the witnesses of the 1919 era: the maids, relatives, theatre employees, chauffeurs, anyone who knew anything about December 2, 1919. It is doubtful whether, in all the history of criminal investigation, such a turn of events could have taken place after so many years. But Roebuck declared that the case had to be probed again in order to clear the Toronto conscience once and for all.

Investigators found a hopelessly tangled case. They heard from some quarters that Theresa had made a confession in 1929 that she contributed to Small's murder and had shown the confession to Sullivan in exchange for the promise that he was to cease his attacks upon her for the remainder of her natural life. Given the promise, she is said to have told Sullivan: "Now you know the truth, leave me to die in peace and then have your fun."

Roebuck was unimpressed. He knew that a man like Sullivan, and the two Small sisters, would never have kept quiet about such a revelation. Yet in his hands was a signed confession and he turned it over to his investigators to be checked out for the writing, the signature, and general contents.

Hundreds of typewriters were checked out by weary sleuths. Notepaper manufacturers such as Warwick Brothers were questioned as to the kind of notepaper that Theresa had purchased, the kind of paper used by Sullivan at the Sovereign Press, the writing-paper the Small sisters used in their correspondence.

To one sleuth, Sullivan remarked: "I hear you're searching

for a typewriter around my place . . . you're getting too damn nosey . . . you'll find yourself in trouble if you don't watch out."

"Out of my way, Sullivan," answered the private eye. "If you're not careful with your words you'll land back in the pokey, . . . you were there once before because you opened your big mouth."

"The true reason for my imprisonment," shouted Sullivan, loud enough for the ever-present press to hear, "was to completely cover up the murder of Small—the unsolved case that brands the authorities of Ontario lower than a snake's belly."

It made the front pages.

One of the persons whom investigators were seeking was Hilda Weiss, formerly a maid of Theresa's. It was the Toronto *Telegram* that found her, in California.

"The Small house was haunted," she said. "The chauffeur and I used to hear strange noises all through the night. I was always scared. When Mr. Small didn't come home that night, I saw Mrs. Small sneak down to the basement at two o'clock to pray."

"Was she alone?"

"No, she came up with her priest," she replied. "Mrs. Small had two locked rooms in the cellar. She carried the keys with her. Even when she went to the hospital after an accident, she had them with her. And Mrs. Small never went to the basement without her rosary. It was all so scary. I finally left because I was afraid to spend another night in the place."

"Did you ever see other people at the house, other than Mrs. Small's close personal friends, nuns, priests, and members of the family?"

"The staff were given orders never to let anyone into the house unless they were known to us as friends of the missus. She said she had too many enemies and some of them were detectives. I would tell people that Mrs. Small was not at home while she would stand in the darkness at the top of the landing and watch."

"What did Mrs. Small do, if anything, that seemed unusually strange when her husband failed to come home?" the maid was asked.

"She cleaned out all memories of Mr. Small. She threw out his clothes, his pipes and his photographs," concluded Miss Weiss amid the noise of exploding flash powder.

Next came Catherine Dunn, the cook. She recalled that on the night that Ambrose failed to come home not a single person came to the estate on Glen Road. "And I was up until after eleven o'clock," she recalled.

A nurse who had attended Theresa Small during most of her long illness denied that she had ever talked to Sullivan or had ever intimated that the widow had made a death-bed statement. She said that Sullivan was a liar, which was hardly news at any time.

The government investigators as well as the private sleuths were getting nowhere. Many of the important witnesses had been removed by death. Yet, there was one irritating charge that still had to be cleared up to the satisfaction of the clamouring press and the Attorney General's Department. That was the charge by Sullivan and the sisters, that notices asking for prayers for Small's departed soul had been posted in two Toronto convents before the magnate was even reported missing. And this allegation bore some rather strange fruit.

Government sleuths found again that cloistered areas were forbidden to every person except for those mentioned earlier, the doctors, dentists, electricians and so on. But the question recurred: if all these could gain entrance, why not Theresa Small? She had built the convent for the Sisters of Service herself. She used to sit for hours teaching them to sew.

Theresa counselled them when they needed advice. She

attended them in sickness and never failed to show up at the funerals of her favourite nuns. She had contributed lavishly to the convents and novitiates and was generous with gifts and money to the nuns who were old and infirm. She could wander anywhere in the convents that she supported, without question. She could have posted the notices herself.

But in red ink that was the colour of blood? Investigators couldn't bring themselves to believe that a woman like Theresa, kind and generous, always thinking of others, particularly the poor, the old and the very young, could commit such an act.

Thousands of man-hours were utilized in the probe of Theresa's personality, her family ties, her friends, in an attempt to find some flaw in her character or temperament. The results were disclosed in a lengthy document that was presented to Attorney General Roebuck on August 10, 1936. Roebuck and his staff studied the report for two months and then submitted it to the Ontario Supreme Court for a decision. Mr. Justice Jeffery ruled the confession a forgery and threw the entire case out of court.

"All evidence shows," he said, "that Mrs. Small was a good and charitable woman and not a tittle of evidence has come forward that she had anything whatsoever to do with the disappearance of her husband."

This ended the Small case as far as the courts were concerned, but Toronto police decided to keep it on the active file, "just in case." Mitchell continued in charge and as late as the mid-1940's he was still digging, but instead of the Rosedale Ravine he had switched his efforts to the site of an abandoned piggery in East York. The Criminal Investigation Bureau of the Ontario Provincial Police erased the files on Small but would be called back into the mystery within another three years.

Chapter Fourteen

In July, 1939, Gertrude Small left the sisters' new home on Dovercourt Road in Toronto and took residence in Midland, to be near the Martyrs' Shrine. Someone had told her that only prayers at this shrine could cure a nervous affliction from which she was suffering, a disease that was causing her hands and face to twitch spasmodically.

During the summer months in Midland she appeared at the shrine at regular intervals where she prayed at a church which had been denied her by her father half a century before. She told a companion that she had improved dramatically from her shrine visits and that she intended to spend the rest of her years at Midland.

While staying at the Georgian Hotel in Midland, she met Warren Gordon Bell, a town electrician who had been sent to her room by the hotel to repair some electrical fixtures. Bell was thirty-nine and he apparently saw in Gertrude a vision of his late mother. The two began seeing each other on a regular basis.

Bell's past was uncomplicated. Born in New Lowell, a tiny village near Barrie, Ontario, he was a devoted son to a fawning mother and he remained dutifully at her side while the other members of the family followed their natural instincts and were married. He had six sisters and was constantly pampered by them until they left home.

By 1939 his mother was dead and Bell, perhaps needing the comfort of a new mother, turned to Gertrude Small. She was fifty-five and grey-haired. They were seen walking occasionally together during the sunny month of August and then more frequently in September, when Gertrude returned to Toronto briefly to introduce Bell to Florence and to Patrick Sullivan, who was still living with her.

Both disliked Bell instantly. They could not understand why a man sixteen years younger than Gertrude could be overwhelmed by love and interested in marriage. It just didn't add up. Florence, as usual, agreed with Sullivan's character-assassination. She thought there was something fishy in the relationship. She apparently said so, insulting Warren Bell and sending the two back to Midland.

Sullivan, always the master of innuendo and half-truth, presumed that Bell was a Catholic and had lured Gertrude back to the church of her early years. He heaped vilifications on Bell by a constant barrage of letters to Gertrude and demanded that she stop seeing him.

What Florence and Patrick didn't know was that Bell was a Presbyterian and had no connection whatsoever with the Catholic Church or the Martyrs' Shrine at Midland. He and Gertrude laughed at Sullivan's continuous verbal venom and kept the whole thing a secret.

But Sullivan, unchanged in fifteen years, believed himself a super sleuth and travelled to Midland to snoop into the life and affairs of Bell. He found that Bell was signing his meals at the hotel and that Gertrude was paying for them out of her monthly allowance from the Small estate.

But all the sleuthing and squabbling was to no avail. On Thursday, October 26, the couple drove in Warren's car from Midland to Stayner, a hop of twenty-five miles, and there in the presence of two witnesses, Captain Alexander Colquhoun and his wife, Warren and Gertrude tied the knot.

Investigation by provincial police a short time later revealed that the couple had had difficulty getting someone to marry them. Gertrude had signed her marriage certificate as a Roman Catholic and refused to permit a United Church minister in Stayner to marry her, as the United Church had been particularly unhelpful in the campaign against Theresa Small. Finally, a telephone call to the adjacent village of Duntroon brought the Reverend J. W. Downer of the Church of England to the Wilcox Inn at Stayner, and at 7:45 p.m., after more than two hours' delay in their plans, the couple were married and left for Midland and their honeymoon.

While short-cutting across Wasaga Beach, along a stretch of hard sand barely discernible in the gathering fog of the fall evening, Bell drove his car off the surface of the sand road in the vicinity of the Nottawasaga River. Captain Colquhoun and his wife, following the fast-stepping couple, lost the car's rear lights in the fog and were unable to locate them thereafter.

The automobile had plunged into eight feet of water. Gertrude was trapped in the front seat, partly under the dashboard, and Warren, apparently freed of the car, was carried away into Georgian Bay.

It was in the morning of October 27 that someone saw the car gleaming in the sun in the Nottawasaga River. Gertrude's body was recovered a short time later. It was not until three in the afternoon that Bell's body was found by duck-hunters, three miles eastward on the bay shore.

The news of the tragedy occurring a few minutes after a marriage would have made front-page news anywhere in Canada. But when it was discovered that the bride was none other than Gertrude Small, headlines blazed across the tops of the national and international dailies. It was given impetus by Florence who screamed to reporters: "I don't give a damn who knows it . . . but my sister was murdered."

"Very fishy indeed," said Sullivan. And both of them headed for Wasaga Beach to investigate.

To compound the mystery of the case, a country coroner near Wasaga Beach decided that Gertrude had died of shock and released the body for burial. A local police constable told the press that her body had been wedged tightly under the dash and she was in a kneeling position, which was a natural position after such a crash. However, the press made a controversy over the situation, stating that Bell apparently escaped from his car through a rip in the convertible roof. Why he had not been able to reach shore, only a few feet from where the car entered the water, was inexplicable.

No one could fathom why Bell's body was found three miles from the scene. Also, why had a coroner decided that Gertrude's death was caused by shock?

"What the hell is shock?" asked Florence Small. She raced to the Attorney General's office in Toronto and demanded of the incumbent, Arthur Conant, a full provincial investigation. Conant was sympathetic. He too had been perturbed by the report of shock and had wondered if Gertrude Small had been drugged. In his position, he could ill afford to allow the case to go unsolved.

While Conant was discussing the affair with others of his department and with the provincial crime laboratory, he received a letter from Florence Small, a letter that reached the Toronto dailies at the same time that he received it.

Dear Mr. Conant:
Re: The death of my sister, Miss Gertrude Small.
Please inform me when her inquest will be held but not until next week in order to give Mr. Pat Sullivan, an old friend of my sister and I, an opportunity to investigate all the surroundings of my sister's death. I request, too, that

*Mr. Sullivan be permitted to cross-examine all witnesses at
the inquest in the interests of justice, law and order.*

Florence Small.
349 Dovercourt Road, Toronto.

Conant acted immediately. He sent to Midland Dr. E. C.
Fielden, one of the leading pathologists in the country, to
determine the cause of death. Then he sent Dr. E. R. Frankish, the department's chief medico-legal expert, to determine
if there had been a crime, a drowning with drug involvement,
or some other cause of death.

Toronto police were in no way involved. And to be "on the
safe side," in case there was foul play, the Provincial Police sent
Inspector Hammond, who had helped bungle the long years of
investigation of the Ambrose Small case.

A parade of witnesses told of seeing a car racing eastward
along the beach that night, shortly after nine o'clock, about the
time that Warren and Gertrude would be travelling through
the fog. Some of them thought it would be simple for a driver
unfamiliar with the beach at the turn over the Nottawasaga
River to miss the bridge and plunge into the river.

But how Bell got out and was carried for three miles to a
lonely shoreline was not clear. One reporter guessed that Bell
had escaped the plunge into the river, then jumped back in to
rescue Gertrude but was carried away by the current. Another
group of reporters found that the river had little or no current
at that time of year. Had Bell escaped and wandered along the
beach, finally plunging into the water and drowning?

The story could not be pieced together and Hammond was
of little help. One thing was certain, however: both pathologists said that Gertrude died of drowning.

"There was water in her lungs," said Dr. Fielden.

"She did not die of shock," said Dr. Frankish, "and no foul play is indicated."

The double drowning had no connection with the disappearance of Ambrose Small. All it did was to reopen the old mystery in the pages of the daily newspapers, an indication that the case was not forgotten. It was, however, still on the active file of the Toronto Police Department where it would remain for another twenty years.

In May 1944 the old Grand Opera House was levelled to make way for a service station and parking lot. As a giant crane with a battering ram of concrete and steel slammed against the dull red-brick walls and ripped apart the sturdy beams of oak, a small crowd of spectators stood vigil each day. Truckloads of rubble groaned out of the laneway but pieces of twisted ironwork from the once-ornate entrance were carried away by souvenir hunters.

A week passed by and the walls and floors had disappeared. Only the concrete floor of the basement and furnace room remained. This would have ordinarily been filled with the rubble from the upper structure and smoothed over with earth and new concrete but for one reason. Austin Mitchell, now an inspector and soon to be retired, was on the scene and wanted to have a look beneath the furnace-room floor. It had been dug up and replaced many years before, but why let a last chance go by without another look.

The shovel tore at the thick concrete and unloosed it from the clay base. Mitchell went down the side of the wall. The small crowd peered over the brink. There was nothing beneath the floor, no bones, no ashes, nothing except brown clay which had not been disturbed for a century.

This may have been the final curtain in the drama that had played to an entire generation. But who can be sure? The ghosts of this bizarre case have never rested easily.